400 Jokes

You Can Tell

Anybody

Compiled by: **Brian Keelan**

ISBN ISBN-13: 978-1511942317
ISBN-10: 1511942312

Foreword

First of all, thanks for buying my book.

When you are reading this book, take your time. There is a lot of good material here that will not just make you laugh but will also make the people you tell them to laugh... if you tell them in the right way and in the right circumstance.

You will also find this material comes in handy for speech writing.

A friend of mine, who had purchased my first joke book for a friend of his, showed me a copy of the letter his friend had written to thank him.

He wrote:

"When I saw what kind of book it was, I decided to ration myself to one joke a day or two short ones, with rereads in order to maximize the pleasure. I finished it in November and now I am ready to pass judgement.

It is without a doubt the best book of jokes I have ever read.

Your friend Brian has done a terrific job of editing some old blisters, and there's a lot of material which is new to me. Thanks for sending me a copy.

It's part of my front-and-center library, ready for referencing on a moment's notice."

That is exactly what I was going for.

This is the 2nd edition of this version of the book and has over 200 new jokes in it along with most of the classics from the first book.

Please enjoy and if perchance you happen to come across any good ones that I may have missed, please send them along to my contact list at: www.briankeelan.com

Table of Contents

Chapter 1 – Just plain funny – 1

Chapter 3 – Legal, political & corporate – 37

Chapter 4 – Fast thinkers – 61

Chapter 5 – Men vs. Women – 79

Chapter 6 – Drinking stories – 99

Chapter 7 – Multi-cultural – 113

Chapter 8 – Senior moments – 151

Bonus Chapter – Paraprasdokians – 167

About the author – 172

The Joke Book app – 173

Other Works – 174

Chapter 1

Just Plain Funny

The cowboy and his bible

A devout cowboy lost his favorite Bible while he was mending fences out on the range.

Three weeks later a cow walked up to him carrying the Bible in its mouth. The cowboy couldn't believe his eyes. He took the precious book out of the cow's mouth, raised his eyes to heaven and cried out, "It's a miracle!"

"Not really," said the cow. "Your name is written right inside the cover."

Grampa takes Johnny out for lunch

When Grampa picks Johnny up to go to lunch together, he asks him, "Where would you like to eat Johnny?"

Johnny says, "Can we go to MacDonald's?"

Grampa, deciding to make this interesting, tells Johnny, "I'll tell you what kiddo. If you can spell MacDonald's, we'll go there."

Johnny replies, "Awww… the heck with that. Let's just go to KFC."

Ultimate Good News / Bad News

After an operation to have one of his legs amputated, a man wakes up and is told by the doctor that he has some good news and some bad news for him.

"Give me the bad news first please?"

The doctor tells him, "The bad news is that we made a huge mistake in the operating room and amputated the wrong leg."

The patient is dumbstruck and struggles to ask, "What could possibly be considered good news after terrible news like that?"

The smiling doctor tells him, "Well, the good news is that it looks like your other leg is getting better."

Bad news and then… more bad news

A man decides to take up skydiving. He enrolls in the course, goes to all the lessons and even does his simulated tower jump. At last the big day arrives and he is ready for his first real parachute jump.

But, at forty five hundred feet, just as he approaches the door to jump, he recoils in horror and fear at the sight. He tells the instructor, "I can't do this. I'll die if I do. I just can't do it!"

The instructor calms him down. "Don't be afraid. Think about it now...you've rehearsed this over one hundred times. All you've got to do is step out of the plane, count to three and pull the ripcord. If nothing happens count to three again and pull the emergency cord.

There is a pickup truck down there waiting for you with a nice cold beer. It's easy... a walk in the park. Come on man... let's do this!"

Encouraged by this, the guy jumps... counts to three and pulls the ripcord and nothing happens.

He counts to three again and pulls the emergency cord.

Again, nothing happens.

As he plummets to his death, he says to himself, "What a rip-off! I'll bet that stupid beer truck isn't waiting down there either."

How Johnny learned to count

When the teacher asks Johnny if he knows how to count, he replies, "Yes I do ma'am. My father taught me."

Pleased to hear that, the teacher says, "That's wonderful Johnny. Now then, can you please tell us what number comes after three?"

An angelic looking Johnny replies, "Four."

The teacher says, "That's right! Very good Johnny! Now can you tell us all what number comes after six?"

"Seven."

"Way to go Johnny!" says the teacher with a big smile. "Your father has done a fantastic job. Now, please tell us what comes after ten?"

A smiling Johnny replies, "The Jack."

Johnny learns to multiply

Little Johnny came home from school looking very upset. When his father asked him why, Johnny told him it was because he'd gotten kicked out of math class.

"What happened?" asked the father.

Johnny said, "It all got started when the teacher asked me, how much is two times three and I said six."

"But that's right!" exclaimed his father.

"Then she asked me how much is three times two," he went on.

"Two times three, three times two, what the hell is the difference?" asked his father.

Johnny replied, "That's exactly what I said!!"

How Johnny drives teachers crazy # 1

Teacher: "Johnny, your essay titled: 'My Dog' is exactly the same as your brother's. Can you please explain this?"

Johnny: "Duhhh… hello Miss Jones… it's the same dog."

How Johnny drives teachers crazy # 2

Teacher: "Johnny, what do you call a person who keeps on talking when people are no longer interested?"

Johnny: "A teacher."

How Johnny drives teachers crazy # 3

Teacher: "Johnny, what do your mom and dad have in common?"

Johnny: "Neither of them want any more kids."

How Johnny drives teachers crazy # 4

Teacher: "Johnny, how can you tell if two people are married?"

Johnny: "They're both yelling at the same kids."

How Johnny drives teachers crazy # 5

When asked by his teacher why he was wearing a Medical Alert bracelet, Johnny replied, "I'm allergic to nuts and eggs."

The teacher asked, "Are you allergic to cats?"

Johnny replied, "I don't know... I don't eat cats."

How Johnny drives teachers crazy # 6

The math teacher asks Johnny, "If you have five candies and your sister asks for one, how many will you have left?"

A smiling Johnny replies, "Five."

Johnny learns to hunt

Its summer and Johnny is visiting his uncle's farm. During the first three days, the uncle showed him all the usual things; chickens, cows, crops, farm machinery, etc. After that, Johnny's uncle sensed that Johnny was getting bored and he was running out of things with which to amuse him.

Then he had an idea. "Johnny, there's no one around for miles, why don't you grab a gun, take the dogs, and go shooting?"

Johnny was quite enthusiastic about that idea and soon he and the dogs were on their way.

A few hours later, Johnny returned and his uncle asked him, "Well… how did you like that?"

"That was great!" exclaimed a smiling Johnny. "Have you got any more dogs?"

Setting a standard for your kids

A father who was trying to motivate his son to study, said to him, "You know, when Abe Lincoln was your age, he was studying books by the light of the fireplace."

The son replied, "Really? Well thanks for sharing that with me dad but… did you know that when Abe Lincoln was your age, he was President of the United Sates?"

Cast Away

From the observation deck of a passenger ship, everyone can see a very small, deserted island with only one palm tree. On the island, beside the tree, is a man wearing only a pair of tattered pants. He is jumping up and down; shouting and desperately waving his hands.

"Who's that?" a passenger asks the captain.

The captain replies, "I have no idea. But every year when we pass this little island, he just goes nuts."

21st century discipline

Two fathers are having a beer at the local pub and one complains, "When I was a youngster, my parents would punish me by sending me to my room without supper. Today my son has his own flat-screen TV, phone, a computer with internet hook-up and an Xbox with lots games in his room."

"So what do you do to punish him?" asked his friend.

"I send him to my room!"

Fire trucks

When a fire started on some grassland near a farm in Indiana, the fire department from the nearby town was called to put the fire out. When the fire proved to be more than the town fire department could handle so a smaller, rural, volunteer fire department was called to provide additional manpower.

Soon, the smaller volunteer fire department arrived in a dilapidated old fire truck which they proceeded to drive straight into the middle of the flames and stop. Once it had stopped, all the volunteer firemen jumped off the truck and frantically started stamping out the flames and spraying water in all directions. Soon they had snuffed out the center of the fire, breaking the blaze into two easily controllable parts which were then extinguished..

The farmer was so impressed by the volunteer fire department's bravery and hard work as well as grateful to them for saving his farm, that he presented the volunteer fire department with a check for $5,000.

A local news reporter asked what the fire department captain would do with the funds.

"That should be quite obvious," he responded. "The very first thing we're gonna do is get the brakes on that stupid truck fixed!"

The blonde astronomer

A hot-looking blonde gets invited to a faculty party at the university where she meets a handsome astronomy professor.

Wanting to make a good impression, she tells him, "Okay now… I've figured out how you guys determine the size of the star and what their distance from earth is. What I can't figure out is how you find out what their names are."

The blonde and the used car

This blonde is not having very good luck trying to sell her car. That's because it has over 250,000 miles on it.

A brunette friend told her, "I have a friend who can help you solve your problem. He owns a repair shop and if you tell him that I sent you and then ask him to turn your odometer back to 50,000 miles, he'll do it.

Then it shouldn't be a problem to sell your car."

The next day, the blonde took her car to her friend's mechanic and had the work done.

A month later, the blonde ran into the brunette who asked her if she had sold her car yet.

The blonde replied, "Heck no! Why would I do that? It only has 50,000 miles on it."

Two snakes are talking

One snake turns to his buddy in a panic and asks, "Are we poisonous?"

His buddy says, "Yes we most certainly are. Is there a problem?"

The first snake says, "I'm afraid so. I just bit my tongue."

Two snowmen are standing in the front yard.

One of them turns to the other and asks, "Do you smell carrots?"

8 Questions your kids will love

1: What's the difference between roast beef and pea soup?

    A: Anyone can roast beef.

2: Why do cows wear bells?

    A: Because their horns don't work.

3: Why are there so many Smiths in the phone book?

    A: They all have phones.

4: Mary's father has five daughters. Their names are: Nini, Nana, Nora and Nunu. What it the name of the 5th daughter?

    A: Mary.

5: Where does a five hundred pound canary sleep?

    A: Anywhere it wants to.

6: Why don't blind people skydive?

    A: It scares the daylights out of the dog.

7: What's the difference between snot and cauliflower?

    A: Kids will eat snot.

8: What's green and hangs from trees?

    A: Giraffe snot.

A blonde in the office

A man named Smith who worked in a very high pressure call center was quite stressed and in urgent need of a few days off work. He knew the boss—a real task master—would not allow him to leave unless he had a great excuse so he came up with the idea that maybe if he acted like he was cracking up under all the stress, the boss would send him home for a few days.

So, he hung upside down from the ceiling fan yelling, "Whee! Look at me! I'm a lightbulb!" and making funny, crackling noises.

Miss Jones, a blonde who worked in the cubicle beside him asked him what he was doing and he told her he was pretending to be a light bulb so that the boss would think he was cracking up under all the pressure and give him a few days off.

A few minutes later the boss came into the office and asked him, "Smith! What the heck do you think you are doing there?"

Smith told his boss, "Can't you tell? I'm a fluorescent light bulb!"

His boss told him, "You are clearly cracking up Smith. I think you should go home and recuperate for a couple of days… and don't come back until you're feeling better! I don't want to hear any more of that light bulb crap when you come back. Do you understand?"

Smith said, "Yes sir!" as he jumped down, put his coat on and headed for the door.

Miss Jones, upon seeing this, picked up her stuff and started to follow him out.

The boss asked her, "And just where do you think you're going Miss Jones?"

She told him, "I'm going home, too. I can't work in the dark."

A blonde learns how to fix her car

A blonde pushes her BMW into a gas station and tells the mechanic it just died. After working on it for a few minutes, he has it idling smoothly.

"What was the problem?" she asks.

He tells her, "Just crap in the carburetor."

With a look of disgust she says, "Eeewww? Yuck! How often do I have to do that?"

A blonde goes to her doctor

A gorgeous young redhead goes to see her doctor claiming that her body hurt wherever she touched it.

"That's not possible!" says the doctor. "Show me."

The redhead took her finger, pushed on her left shoulder and screamed then she pushed her elbow and screamed even more. She pushed her knee and screamed and then she pushed her ankle and screamed. Everywhere she touched made her scream.

The doctor said, "You're not really a redhead, are you?"

"Well, no," she said, "I'm actually a natural blonde."

"I thought so," the doctor said.

"What makes you think that?" she asked.

He told her, "You have a broken finger my dear."

Kindergarten follies

It was the last day of kindergarten and all the kids brought a present for their teacher, the very lovely Miss Jones.

When the florist's son handed Miss Jones her present, she noticed the aroma of flowers and held it up saying, "I'll bet I know what's in here – flowers."

"That's right," the little boy said.

Then the candy-store owner's daughter handed Miss Jones a gift.

She held it up, shook it and said, "I'll bet I know what this is. It's a box of candy."

"That's right!" the little girl shouted with glee.

The next gift was from the son of the local party-store owner. Miss Jones held it up and noticed that it was leaking so she touched a drop with her finger and put it on her tongue.

"Is it white wine?" she asked.

"No," the boy answered.

She touched another drop and put some more on her tongue in order to get a better taste.

"Is it champagne?" she asked.

"Wrong again," the boy answered.

The teacher tasted it again and then, unable to guess what it might be, said, "I give up. What is it?"

The smiling, excited little boy replied, "It's a puppy!"

The difference between anger and exasperation

Johnny comes home from school one day and tells his father that he has a tough homework assignment from school: "I need to be able to explain the difference between anger and exasperation."

The Dad replies, "Not to worry my son… it's really only a matter of degree. Here, I'll show you."

He picks up the phone, dials a number at random and when a man answers he asks, "Hello, is Marv there?"

The man answers, "I'm sorry but there is no one here by that name.

You must have a wrong number."

The father says, "Sorry," and hangs up.

Then he says, "OK Johnny, now watch and I'm going to demonstrate for you what anger is."

He dials the same number again and when the same guy answers, he says, "Hi, is Marv there?"

"Now listen mister, you just called this number and I told you there is no one here by that name! Now look up the friggin' number in the book and stop calling me!" Then he slammed the receiver down.

The father says, "Okay Johnny... that was anger. Now I'll demonstrate for you what exasperation is."

With that he picked up the phone and dialed the same number again. A very angry voice answered the phone and yelled, "What!!!"

Johnny's father, very calmly said, "Hi, this is Marv calling. I'm wondering if there have been any calls for me?"

Smoke signals

Two guys are installing a living room, wall-to-wall carpet for a lady. At coffee-break time, one of the installers went outside for a smoke only to discover that he'd lost his cigarettes.

When he went back into the living room, he noticed a small lump under the carpet. Assuming the smokes fell out of his pocket and not wanting to rip up the entire carpet for a pack of smokes; he took his rubber mallet out and proceeded to flatten the carpet in order to hide his cigarettes.

As he is cleaning up before leaving, the lady of the house comes in to pay him. She hands him his cheque and says, "Oh, by the way... here are your cigarettes. You must have dropped them in the driveway."

He thanks her and turns to leave as she asks, "By the way, I don't suppose you've seen my pet hamster running around here have you?"

Be careful what you say in front of your kids

The young couple invited their elderly pastor to join them for Sunday dinner. While they were in the kitchen preparing the meal, the minister asked their son what they were having for dinner.

"Goat," the little boy replied.

"Goat!" replied the startled man of the cloth. "Are you sure about that?"

"I certainly am," said the youngster. "This morning, I heard my dad tell my mom, 'Today is just as good a day as any to have that old goat for dinner.'"

A classy complaint

A guest in a posh hotel called over the head waiter one morning and gave him his order for breakfast, "I'd like one under-cooked egg so that it's nice and runny, and one very over-cooked egg; you know... tough and hard. With that I want three strips of barely grilled bacon, a bit on the cold side along with some burnt toast. On the side I'd like some butter straight from the freezer so that it's impossible to spread and rips the toast to shreds, along with a pot of very weak, lukewarm coffee."

"That's a pretty complicated order sir," said the bewildered waiter. "It might be quite difficult to provide it just as you asked."

The guest replied sarcastically, "Well... it can't be that difficult because that's exactly what you brought me yesterday!"

The egotistical specialist

A patient nervously enters the examination room of a famous specialist who asks him, "So who did you see before coming to me?"

The patient answered, "My family general practitioner."

"Your GP!" scoffed the doctor. "What a waste of time and money! What sort of useless, stupid advice did he give you?"

The patient replied, "He advised me... to come and see you."

Why did the blonde climb over the glass wall?

A: To see what was on the other side.

Stewart Francis on spelling

"So what if I can't spell Armageddon?

It's not the end of the world."

The job interview

A young engineer, fresh out of college, was interviewing for a job at a large pharmaceutical company. The interviewer asked him, "What starting salary are you thinking about?"

The graduate earnestly replied, "I'd really like to get something in the $100,000 a year range."

The interviewer tells him, "What would you say to a salary of $100,000, five weeks of vacation, fourteen paid holidays, a company matching retirement fund to fifty per cent of your salary, full medical and dental and a company car every two years... say a BMW?"

The stunned graduate replied, "Wow, you must be kidding man."

The smiling interviewer said, "Of course I am, but you started it."

One for the National Wildlife Federation

A forest ranger catches a man in the woods; cooking and eating a bald eagle. He is arrested, charged and goes to court where he pleads guilty but claims extenuating circumstances.

"It's like this your honor. I got lost in the woods and hadn't eaten for three days. I'm at this lake and I see a bald eagle swooping down to catch a fish. I take my bow and arrow and try to shoot the fish out of the eagle's claws but unfortunately, I killed the eagle. Since he was dead anyway and I was starving, I decided to eat him figuring that it would be a waste to just let him rot there."

After taking a recess to deliberate, the judge returned and said, "Due to the extreme nature of your circumstance, the court will dismiss the charge. However, would you please satisfy the court's curiosity by describing to the court what a bald eagle tastes like?"

The man says, "Well your honor, the closest I could come would be to say that it tastes a lot like a combination of a Spotted Owl and a California Condor."

A blonde plays Trivial Pursuit

A blonde was playing Trivial Pursuit and it was her turn. She rolled the dice and landed on the Science & Nature category. Her question was: "If you are in a vacuum and someone calls your name, can you hear it?"

She thought for a time and then asked, "Is it on or off?"

Some compassion for O.J.

A guy driving to work on the freeway in Los Angeles runs into heavy traffic that soon comes to a complete standstill in a classic L.A. gridlock. While sitting there in his car, he notices that up ahead there is a man running from car to car... talking with each of the drivers.

When the man gets to his car, he tells him, "O.J. Simpson is up at the head of this traffic jam and he's pretty upset about having to give eight and a half million dollars to the Goldman family. He says if he can't raise the money, he's going to douse himself in gasoline and set himself on fire. I'm going around to each car asking for donations."

The guy in the car, reaching for his wallet, says, "OK, I'm in." Then he asks, "How much do you have?"

The man says, "Almost ten gallons."

Who's really doin' who?

There's a little fellow named Junior who hangs out at a local grocery store. The owner doesn't know what Junior's problem is, but he notices that the boys like to tease him. They say he is a, "few bricks shy of a load." To prove it, they would sometimes offer Junior his choice between a nickel and a dime. He always takes the nickel; they say, because it's bigger.

One day, after Junior had once again grabbed the nickel, the store owner took him to one side and said, "Junior, those guys are just making fun of you: they think you don't know that the dime is worth more than the nickel. Are you grabbing the nickel just because it's bigger, or what?"

Junior said, "Heck no. I take the nickel because if I took the dime, they'd quit doing it!"

The goat and the railroad tie

Two guys out hunting are walking across a field trying to flush out some pheasant. They come across a hole in the ground that's about eight feet across but, it is so deep that they can't see the bottom. One of the guys drops a rock into it and they listen for a sound but… hear nothing. Next they drop a bigger rock into the hole but still, they don't hear anything.

Now they go and look for something larger and find an old railroad tie. They haul the railroad tie back to the hole and dump it in. Down it goes… and again… no sound.

About thirty seconds later, a goat comes running along doing about sixty miles an hour and dives straight into the hole. They listen… but… still no sound.

A few minutes later, a farmer comes along, "Say, have you fellas seen a goat around here?"

They tell him, "We could hardly believe it but a goat just came running right by us – going like crazy – and it dove right into that deep hole over there."

The farmer replied, "Well then boys, that weren't my goat. My goat was tied to a railroad tie."

Switching trains

Skinner is being interviewed for the position of signalman at his local railroad station. The inspector who is conducting the interview asks him, "What would you do if you had two trains heading toward each other on the same track?"

Skinner tells him, "That's easy. I'd just switch one train over to another track."

"That's good Mr. Skinner. Now tell me what you would do if the switch lever broke?"

"In that case, I'd run down to the tracks and use the manual lever."

"Very good answer Mr. Skinner. Now then, what if you got down to the tracks and found that the manual lever had been struck by lightning and was inoperable?"

"Well if that happened, I'd run back up here to the office and phone the next signal box down the line and tell them to do the switch there."

"Excellent. Now then, what if the phone was out of order?"

"I'd run down to the street and use the pay phone near the station."

"Good thinking Mr. Skinner. But what if that phone had been vandalized?"

"Well then I'd run into town and get my old pal Vern and bring him back to the station."

The puzzled inspector asks him, "Now why would you do that?"

Skinner has an evil grin on his face as he tells them, "Because old Vern's never seen a train wreck before."

A van full of penguins

A cop stops a guy driving a van on the freeway because he noticed that the guy had a whole bunch of penguins in the back.

"And just what the heck is going on here with all these penguins in your van?" the cop asked.

With an exasperated look, the driver replied, "I'm trying to find something to do with all these frigging penguins!"

"Well, I suggest you take them to the zoo," the cop replied.

The guy's face lit up as the lights went on, "An excellent idea officer and thank you so much for your help."

Then he drove away… relieved and smiling.

The next day, the same cop stops the same guy in the same van… still with all the penguins. The only difference is that today, the penguins are all wearing sunglasses.

"I thought I told you to take those penguins to the zoo!"

The driver leaned out the window and said, "Yeah, I know officer. We did that yesterday and they had a great time there. Today we're going to the beach."

The roar of the greasepaint

Fred and Bernie haven't seen each other for years and they meet on the street in New York City. Glad to see each other, they decide to have a beer and catch up.

Fred says, "So Bernie, whatcha doin' these days?"

Bernie replies, "I work in the circus."

"Really. That sounds like fun. What do you do in the circus?"

"Well, at the beginning of the show, they always have a parade right? Well, I'm the guy who walks behind the elephants with a shovel and a bucket and whenever the elephants drop a turd, I scoop up the turd and put it in the bucket."

"Really? Y'a know… that doesn't sound like a very good job."

Bernie nods in agreement. "It's not. It's actually pretty depressing… and the pay is lousy."

"Well then, why don't you quit and look for another job?"

Bernie says, "What are you? Nuts? – Get out of show business!"

The talent agent

A man auditioning for a talent agent tells him, "I have a most unusual act to show you. One that I'm sure it will amaze you."

He jumps up on top of the agent's desk and throws off his overcoat to reveal a weird, burlap superhero costume…. cape and all. Next he pulls out a pair of ski goggles and puts them on. Then he tucks his thumbs under his armpits, starts wildly flapping his arms and jumps off the desk. His fall slows and then he starts to soar upward, turns and swoops and then proceeds to fly – very gracefully – around the room.

After a couple of trips around the room, he flies back and hovers over the desk, then proceeds to gently lower himself back down on to the desktop.

Back on the desk surface, he scoops up his overcoat and puts it back on. Then he takes his goggles off and puts them back in his coat pocket. After gracefully jumping down onto the floor, he takes a dramatic bow and asks the agent, "So then. What do you think of that?"

The agent stares blankly at him for a moment before he finally asks, "That's it? Bird imitations? All you've got is bird imitations?"

A shaggy dog story

A man who went to see "M*A*S*H" at the movies, heard someone a few rows behind him, laughing... a little too loud. He turned around to glare disapprovingly at the guy and was astounded to see that it was not a guy doing the laughing, but rather, a dog – a large, black Labrador Retriever – sitting there beside his master, laughing his brains out.

During the classically funny scene with the football game at the end of the movie, the dog started to laugh so hard that he was rolling in the aisles – laughing uncontrollably.

When the movie ended, the guy gets up and goes back to the dog's master and says, "I'm sorry to bother you man, but I can't believe what I'm seeing here. Your dog is actually laughing."

The man shrugged his shoulders and said, "Well to tell you the truth... I can't believe it either. He hated the book!"

Two cannibals are eating a clown

One of them asks the other, "Does this taste funny to you?"

A Shakespearean classic

McNeeb–an aging veteran, Shakespearean actor–was playing Hamlet in a small town. When he came to the part where he had to deliver the famous soliloquy, he assumed a dramatic, thespian posture, and began: "To be or not to be: that is the question..."

All of a sudden, out of the audience flew a barrage of tomatoes and other fruits and vegetables in various stages of decay.

One particularly large and very rotten tomato hits McNeeb – splat! – right on the side of the head.

Ever the professional, McNeeb stared at the floor as he calmly removed the splattered tomato pieces from his face.

Then he slowly raised his head and mustering what was left of his dignity, he stared out at the audience and said, "Hey! Come on now! Don't blame me. I didn't write this crap!"

A foul-mouthed parrot

Phil received a parrot as a gift. Unfortunately the parrot had a very bad attitude and his vocabulary was even worse. Every word out of the bird's mouth was extremely rude and laced with profanity. Phil tried and tried to change the bird's attitude by setting a good example; always speaking politely and never cursing. Alas it was all to no avail.

Finally Phil got fed up and yelled at the parrot and when the parrot yelled back at him, Phil grabbed the bird and put him in the freezer. After a few minutes of screaming and cursing the parrot suddenly stopped. There was total silence. Not a peep for five long minutes.

Fearing the parrot might be hurt, Phil opened the freezer door and the parrot calmly stepped out saying, "Listen Philip, I'm really sorry about all the trouble I've caused you. There just is no excuse for that kind of bad attitude and language. Please accept my apologies and rest assured that there will be no further problems."

Phil was stunned yet very pleased at this about face by the parrot and was going to ask what had motivated the parrot to change his ways, when the parrot asked him, "Would you mind terribly sir if I were to ask you what the turkey did?"

My favourite joke as a kid

Q: What is the difference between a tavern and an elephant's fart

A: One is a bar room. The other is a ba-room!

Winner of "World's Funniest Joke"

Two guys are out hunting when one of them collapses. His friend runs over to see what is wrong and is alarmed to see that his pal isn't breathing. In a panic, he whips out his cell-phone and dials '911.'

When the operator comes on he gasps, "I'm out here hunting with my friend and he's just collapsed. I think he's dead! What should I do?"

The operator tells him, "Okay now sir… just calm down. I can help. The first thing you need to do is make sure he's really dead."

The guy says, "Okay. Hang on… I'll be right back."

There is a silence followed by what sounds like a gunshot in the distance.

A few seconds later, the guy picks up the phone and says, "Okay. He's really dead. Now what do you want me to do?"

Professional job envy

Late one night, a neurosurgeon was brushing his teeth before he went to bed. Right in the middle of everything, a pipe underneath the sink burst open and the bathroom began to flood.

He ran to the phone and called a plumber who came straight over – even though it was very late at night.

An hour and a half later, the plumber had fixed the problem and he handed the neurosurgeon his bill… for $700!

The neurosurgeon was shocked, "Seven hundred dollars! How can you possibly charge me $700 for that?"

The plumber replied, "Well I charge a hundred dollars for the late-night service call and four hundred dollars an hour for my time.

I was here for an hour and a half, so that's six hundred dollars for my time plus the hundred for the service call and that's how we get to seven hundred dollars."

The neurosurgeon screamed at him, "Four hundred dollars an hour! That's ridiculous! I'll have you know that I am a neurosurgeon and I only get three hundred dollars an hour!"

The plumber said, "Really. Now there's a coincidence. That's what I used to get when I was a neurosurgeon."

A real optimist

A man fell from the forty fourth floor balcony of a high-rise apartment in New York City. As he plummeted to his death a woman, who was on her balcony on the twenty first floor heard him say as he went by and smiled at her, "Well… so far so good."

Army life

The men of Charlie Company had been out in the field on a brutal three week campaign when the Sergeant announced, "Alright men, gather round. I've got some good news and some bad news for you today. The good news is that today we're all going to get a change of underwear."

The troops started cheering at the news.

"Now for the bad news: Smith, you change with Jones. Andrews, you change with Murphy..."

Navy machismo

The Chief Petty Officer noticed a new seaman standing idly and barked at him, "Get your butt over here sailor!"

The sailor hurried over and stood at attention, "Aye aye sir."

"What's your name sailor?" the CPO demanded.

"John, sir," the new seaman replied.

The CPO glared at him, "Look here sailor, I don't know what kind of bleeding-heart pansy crap they're teaching sailors in boot camp nowadays, but I don't call anyone by their first name. You got that?"

"Yes sir," the seaman replied.

The chief scowled. "Good. We don't do that in this man's Navy because it breeds familiarity, and that leads to a breakdown in authority. I refer to my sailors by their last names only; Smith, Jones, Baker... whatever. And you are to refer to me as 'Chief.' Do I make myself clear?"

"Aye, Aye Chief!"

"Very good sailor: now, what is your last name?"

The seaman sighed, "Darling sir. My name is John Darling, Chief."

The Chief scratched his jaw as he thought about that. Then he said, "Right... okay then John... now... here's what I want you to do."

Psychiatric definitions

A pessimist is: someone who believes the glass is half empty.

An optimist is: someone who believes the glass is half full.

An engineer is: someone who thinks the glass is twice as big as it needs to be.

A realist is: someone who thinks the glass is too small.

A neurotic: someone who is totally sane but not real happy about it.

A cynic is: someone who is plagued by a haunting fear that someone, somewhere, may be happier than they are.

A neurotic is: someone who builds castles in the air

A psychotic is: the person who lives in the castle

A psychiatrist is: The guy who collects the rent

A Freudian slip: when you say one thing but mean... your mother... excuse me.... another!

An example of a Freudian slip

How many Freudian psychiatrists does it take to screw in a light bulb?

A: Two. One to screw in the bulb and one to tell my mother to get off my back... I mean... hold the ladder.

Psychiatric "Don't" # 1

A guy visits a psychiatrist because he is feeling very depressed. The psychiatrist asked him a few questions, took some notes and then just sat there... deep in thought. A few minutes later, he said, "I think I know what your problem is. Your problem is that you have very low self-esteem."

With a reassuring smile he added, "I don't see any reason to be too concerned about it though. It's quite common among losers."

Psychiatric "Don't" # 2

A man is pouring out his heart to his psychiatrist, "Doctor, I am so depressed. I was away on business and I finished early so I e-mailed my wife to tell her I'd be home a day early. I get home from the airport and find her in bed with my best friend. I can't believe it. How could she do this to me?"

The psychiatrist tells him, "Well... maybe she didn't get the e-mail."

Psychiatric "Don't" # 3

A man is told by his psychiatrist after their first session, "I can't say for sure at this point what your real problem is but I think it's fair to assume that you're some kind of a whackjob."

Relationship building

A man tells his psychiatrist, "Nobody likes me."

The psychiatrist says, "Why do you think that is?"

The guy says, "How should I know dickbrain?"

Psychiatric customer profiling

A man walks into a psychiatrist's office with a pancake on top of his head, a fried egg on each shoulder, and a strip of bacon draped over each ear. The psychiatrist asks, "What seems to be the problem?"

The guy looks at him very seriously and says, "Well Doc… I'm really worried about my brother."

Paranoia strikes deep

A guy is having a drink with his friend after a visit to his shrink.

He tells him, "My doctor told me I'm paranoid… well, he didn't actually say it, but I could tell he was thinking it."

Paranoia strikes even deeper

As two psychiatrists pass each other on the street and one of them says, "Good morning."

The second psychiatrist nodded and walked on, muttering to himself, "I wonder what he meant by that?"

Psychiatric patient or just plain psycho?

Two guys in a bar are talking about their therapists. One of them says, "My therapist just told me that I have a dysfunctional preoccupation with vengeance."

He drank the last of his beer, slammed the empty bottle down on the counter and with an evil grin he said, "We'll just see about that!"

How many psychiatrists does it take to change a lightbulb?

A: Only one but the lightbulb has really got to want to change.

Therapy or denial?

"I'm in therapy now. I used to be in denial which frankly… costs a lot less."

Psychiatric progress

After a long session with his patient the psychiatrist told him, "Well Marv, I want to congratulate you on the progress you've made."

Marv says, "Progress! What are you nuts? You call this progress? Six months ago I was Napoleon. Now I'm nobody."

The shrinks are gonna love this guy

Two guys sitting at the bar and one asks, "What are you getting your mother for Mother's Day?"

The second guy says, "A bottle of scotch."

The first guy says, "Really? A bottle of scotch? For your mother? That doesn't seem very appropriate."

The second guy says, "Sure it is. According to her, I'm the reason she drinks."

A pig with a wooden leg

Driving along the Arkansas interstate, a man realized that he was seriously low on gas and pulled off at the next exit. After driving a few lonely miles, he spotted a farmhouse and figuring that most farmers had gasoline for their farm equipment he pulled in, went up on the porch and knocked on the door.

An old farmer came to the door and as he did, the screen door opened and the largest pig the man had ever seen in his life walked out onto the porch. It was easily, well over six hundred pounds! One unusual fact, the pig's right front leg was missing and a wooden peg leg was strapped on in its place.

The startled man remarked to the farmer, "Whoa! That's an unusual looking pig you've got there."

The farmer's face reddened with anger as he said, "Hey there mister… now don't you go sayin' nuthin' bad about my pig! That there pig just happens to be the world's finest pig. Why if it weren't for that pig, I wouldn't even be alive today."

He paused to catch his breath and continued, "Just last fall I was out ploughin' the back forty, and on the back turn I hit a soft spot. The left rear wheel of the tractor sank right into the ground and the whole dang tractor tipped right over on top of me! I wuz gonna be crushed to death but that pig saved my life. He heard my screams, broke out of his pen, ran out to where I was, dug the ground out beneath me and dragged me out of there to safety."

After a pause to catch his breath, he continued, "Two years ago, on a cold winter night, some sparks from the fireplace went out of the chimney onto the roof and set the house on fire. That pig broke out of his pen, crashed through the front door, came right up into our bedroom and woke up my wife and me. Then he helped us get out of the house to safety.

"Nosirree boy, don't you dare go and say one bad thing about that there pig. He's the best dang pig in the whole danged world!"

The visitor replied, "Hey man! Take it easy will ya'! I wasn't trying to insult you or your pig. I'm just saying that it's very unusual to see a pig with a wooden leg like yours has."

The farmer replied, "Now just think about it for a second. You get a wonderful pig like that… you don't eat him all at once."

My dog is better than your dog

Skinner, an avid duck hunter, was in the market for a new bird dog. His search ended when he found a dog that could actually walk on water to retrieve a duck.

"This is fantastic!" he said as he eagerly purchased the dog and took him home. He could hardly wait to show his new dog to his lifelong hunting pal, Tattersall; who Skinner secretly hoped, would be quite jealous of his amazing, new dog.

On the opening day of duck season, he invited Tattersall to go hunting with him and as they waited in the duck blind, a flock of ducks flew by. They both fired, and a duck fell.

Skinner's new dog responded instantly and jumped into the water. The dog, however, did not sink into the water. Instead, the dog tiptoed lightly and quickly across the top of the water, gently picked up the bird and brought it back to the blind, barely even getting his paws wet.

Tattersall saw everything but did not say a single word.

On the drive home, Skinner asked his friend, "So how do you like my new dog?"

After a thoughtful pause Tattersall replied, "Great looking dog ya' got there my friend. Smart too. In fact the only problem I see with your dog is that he can't swim."

For the NRA fans

An Arizona Department of Safety Highway Patrol Officer pulled an SUV over because of a faulty taillight. When the officer approached the driver, the man behind the wheel handed over his driver's license, ownership and insurance slip along with a Concealed Weapon Carry Permit.

The officer took all the documents, looked them over and said, "Well... Mr. Woodrowe Skinner... it says here that you have a Concealed Weapon Carry Permit. Tell me sir, do you have any weapons on you at this time?"

Skinner replied, "Yes I do sir. I have a Smith and Wesson 357 Magnum handgun in a hip holster and a Cobra 22 Derringer in my boot."

The officer nodded his head slowly and then asked, "Mr. Skinner, do you have any other weapons in the vehicle?"

Skinner replied, "Yes sir I do. There's a Colt.45 automatic in the glove box, a Mossberg 500-12 gauge shotgun and an AR-15 in the back; locked up along with the ammunition of course."

The officer then asked Skinner if he was driving to or from a shooting range. Skinner assured him he wasn't.

Now the officer bent over, took his sunglasses off, looked right into Skinner's eyes and said, "Mr. Skinner, you're carrying quite a few guns here. If you don't mind, may I ask what it is that you are afraid of?"

Skinner looked the officer right straight in the eye and very calmly and confidently answered, "Nothing!"

A blonde on an airplane

It's a clear day as a Northwest Airlines jet flies over Arizona. The copilot is on the PA - providing passengers with a commentary about the landmarks below; "Coming up on the right, you can see the Meteor Crater, which is a major tourist attraction in northern Arizona. It was formed when a lump of nickel and iron, roughly 150 feet in diameter and weighing 300,000 tons, smashed into the earth at about 40,000 miles an hour, scattering white-hot debris for miles in every direction. The crater it made measures nearly a mile across and is 570 feet deep."

From the cabin, a blonde passenger was heard to exclaim, "Wow! Look at that will you. It just missed the highway!"

The shmuck and the elephant

A man on safari in Africa comes upon an elephant in great pain – due to a giant thorn in its foot. With extreme caution, he approached the elephant and then very calmly and tenderly, removed the thorn.

The elephant gets up and starts to walk away, then stops, turns and stares at the man for a full minute... locking eyes with him. Then the elephant turns and continues on its way.

The man thinks to himself, "If I ever see that elephant again, I wonder if it will remember me?"

A few years later, the man is at a circus back in the States and notices that one of the elephants keeps looking at him... almost like it knows him. This causes the man to wonder, "Could this possibly be the same elephant that I helped so long ago?"

He decides to take a closer look.

With the elephant still giving him the stare-down, the man moves in closer, until he is right up in front of the elephant. They lock eyes and a knowing look seems to cross the elephant's face as it reaches down and picks the man up carefully with its trunk... lifts him high in the air... and then throws him violently to the ground and stomps him to death!

Turns out... it wasn't the same elephant after all.

The guard-parrot

A postman is out delivering on the first day on his new beat. Halfway through the morning he comes upon a gate marked:

"Danger! Beware of the parrot."

He looks up onto the porch and sure enough, sitting there on his perch is a parrot. The parrot looks harmless and figuring it is some kind of a joke, the postman walks up onto the porch to drop the mail in the slot.

Just as he gets to the top of the steps, the parrot squawks, "Okay Brutus... kill!"

Never assume

His request approved, the CNN News photographer called the local airport to charter a plane and was told that a twin-engine plane would be waiting for him at the airport.

Arriving at the airfield, he spotted a plane warming up outside a hanger. He jumped in, slammed the door and shouted, "Let's go!"

The pilot taxied out, swung the plane into the wind and took off.

Once in the air, the photographer instructed the pilot, "Fly over the valley and make a couple of low passes so I can take some pictures of the fires on the hillsides."

"Why?" asked the pilot.

"Because I'm a photographer for CNN," he responded, "and I need to get some close up shots."

The pilot was strangely silent for a moment before he finally said, "I guess it's a little late for me to be asking this question and I've got a very bad feeling that I'm not going to like the answer, but... you're not my flight instructor are you?"

Groucho Marx

"Military justice is to justice what military music is to music."

Gen. George S. Patton

"You don't win a war by dying for your country. You win a war by making the son-of-a-bitch die for his."

Det. John Corey's rules of engagement (by Nelson DeMille)

"Anything worth shooting once, is worth shooting twice"

Wisdom from the military manuals

* If the enemy is in range, so are you.
* Whoever said the pen is mightier than the sword has obviously never encountered automatic weapons.
* Five second fuses only last about three seconds.
* If you see a bomb technician running, try to keep up with him.
* Never shoot a large caliber man with a small caliber bullet!
* If at first you don't succeed, call in an airstrike.
* If it's stupid but it works... it isn't stupid.
* Always remember to pillage *before* you burn
* Never share a foxhole with someone braver than you.
* When the pin is pulled, Mr. Grenade is not our friend.
* Teamwork is essential. It gives them something to shoot at.
* It takes 15,000 casualties to train a major general.
* If your attack is going too well, you are walking into an ambush.
* Never tell a Platoon Sergeant you have nothing to do
* Try to look unimportant. They may be low on ammo.
* Incoming fire has the right of way

Aviation Wisdom

* An optimist invented the airplane.
  A pessimist invented the parachute.
* Experience is something you don't get until just after you need it.
* If something hasn't broken on your helicopter, it's about to.
* Never fly in the same cockpit with someone braver than you.
* The only time you have too much fuel is when you're on fire.
* In a twin engine aircraft the purpose of the second engine is to supply the pilot with enough power to get to the scene of the crash.
* There are only two types of aircraft... fighters and targets.

* Airspeed, altitude and brains: two of them are always needed in order to successfully complete the flight.
* The Piper Cub is the safest airplane in the world. It can just barely kill you.
* There is no reason to fly through a thunderstorm in peacetime.
* You've never been lost until you've been lost at Mach3.
* Never trade luck for skill.
* Weather forecasts are horoscopes with numbers.
* Just remember, if you crash because of the weather, your funeral will be held on a sunny day.
* If a flight is proceeding incredibly well, something was forgotten.
* If you can't afford to do something right, make darn sure you can afford to do it wrong.
* Death is just nature's way of telling you to watch your airspeed.
* He who demands everything that his aircraft can give him is a pilot; he that demands one iota more is a fool.
* Before each flight, make sure that your bladder is empty and your fuel tanks are full
* Only two bad things can happen to a pilot you and one of them will: A: One day you will walk out to the aircraft knowing that it is your last flight or B: you will walk out to the aircraft not knowing that it is your last flight.

Airline service?

On a small budget airline flying from Chicago to Fort Lauderdale, the flight attendant asked one of the passengers seated in coach if he would like some dinner.

With a smile he asked, "That would be nice. What are my choices?"

With a hardhearted look she replied, "Yes or no."

The Federal Aviation Administration story

The US Federal Aviation Administration (FAA) has a rather unique device for testing the strength of windshields on airplanes. It's a gun that launches a dead chicken at a plane's windshield at about the same speed the plane flies. The theory being that if the windshield didn't crack from the carcass impact, it would survive a collision with a bird during flight.

The British asked to use the device to test the windshield on a brand new, hi-speed locomotive they were developing. On the first shot, the ballistic chicken shattered the windshield, went through the engineer's chair, broke an instrument panel and embedded itself in the back wall of the engine cab. The British were stunned and asked the FAA to recheck the test to see if it had been done correctly.

The FAA reviewed the test thoroughly and came back with one recommendation: "Use a thawed chicken."

Top Ten Rules for pilots

1: Every takeoff is optional. Every landing is mandatory.

2: Flying isn't dangerous. It's the crashing part that's dangerous.

3: The only time you have too much fuel is when you're on fire.

4: A 'good' landing is one from which you can walk away. A 'great' landing is one after which they can use the plane again.

5: Never let an aircraft take you somewhere your brain didn't get to five minutes earlier.

6: Always try to keep the number of landings you make equal to the number of take-offs you've made.

7: Helicopters can't fly; they're just so ugly the earth repels them

8: In the ongoing battle between objects made of aluminum going hundreds of miles per hour and the ground going zero miles per hour, the ground has yet to lose.

9: It is inadvisable to eject directly over the area you just bombed.

10: There are old pilots and there are bold pilots. There are, however, not very many old, bold pilots.

What is the similarity between air traffic controllers and pilots?

A: If a pilot screws up, the pilot dies. If the air traffic controller screws up, the pilot dies.

The FAA (Federal Aviation Administration) motto

We're not happy till you're not happy.

The mechanic and the cardiologist

A Lexus mechanic was removing a cylinder head from the motor of a LS460 when he spotted a well-known cardiologist in his shop. The cardiologist was there waiting for the service manager to come and take a look at his car when the mechanic shouted across the garage,

"Hey Doc, take a look at this?"

The cardiologist, a bit surprised, walked over to where the mechanic was working. The mechanic straightened up, wiped his hands on a rag and asked, "So Doc, look at this engine. I opened its heart, took the valves out, repaired or replaced anything damaged, put everything back in, and when I finished, it worked just like new.

So how is it that I make $48,000 a year and you make $1.7 million when you and I are basically doing the same work?"

The cardiologist paused, leaned over, and then whispered to the mechanic, "Try doing it with the engine running."

Anger management

A man on a train from Chicago to New Orleans told the porter who was checking his compartment for a wake-up call that he wasn't even going to sleep that night. When the porter asked him why not, he said, "Because I'm afraid I'll miss my 6 am stop in Winona Mississippi and it's most important that I get off there since I have a very important sales call to make in the morning."

The porter said, "Well then you don't have a problem sir. That's why I'm here. I'll wake you up in plenty of time to get off in Winona, and I'll even put a nice fresh cup of hot coffee in your hand to get you off to the right start."

The man shook his head saying, "I'm afraid you don't quite understand sir. You see, I have been known to be very difficult to wake up, and if you should call me and I don't wake up, and then you shake me in an effort to try and wake me up, I have been known to come up fighting."

The porter smiled at him and said, "You still don't have a problem sir. I have been a porter on this train for 25 years. I fight with somebody just about every day. But I will guarantee you one thing sir… if you tell me to put you off the train in Winona, I'll put you off the train in Winona! Guaranteed!"

Well, the man felt pretty good about that, so he went to bed and slept like a baby. When he woke up the next morning, the train was stopped. He looked out the window and saw that the train was in Camden, Mississippi: two hours south of Winona!

He exploded in a fit of rage and burst out of his sleeping compartment yelling, screaming and swearing at everyone in his path.

He found the porter and started beating, punching, cussing, and scrapping with him. Anybody who tried to help the porter came under his wrath.

Another porter called the police and ultimately, four policemen managed to overpower him. They hauled him off the train and out into the parking lot… still cussing, fighting and hollering.

When they had finally subdued him, they called the president of the railroad, told him what had happened and asked, "What do you want us to do here? We've got a maniac on our hands!"

"Well it's your fault," the president said. "You're the ones that didn't wake him up. Now, you give him the money he lost by not getting off in Winona and put him on the next train north - NOW!"

So, they calmed him down, paid him off and got him on the next train north. As the train was pulling out of the station, one of the porters, who was wiping the blood and sweat off of his face and neck said to the other porter, "Man. That was just about the maddest human being I have ever seen in my life. Wouldn't you agree?"

The other porter said, "Well, I will admit, he was a pretty mad fellow, but I have to tell you that in my lifetime, I actually have seen one man even madder than him."

"Who could that possibly be?" the other porter asked.

"The man I put off the train this morning in Winona."

The golden age of insults

Mae West
"His mother should have thrown him away and kept the stork."

Eddie Cantor: "He hasn't an enemy in the world… but all his friends hate him."

Mark Twain: "I didn't attend the funeral, but I sent a nice letter saying I approved of it."

Rodney Dangerfield: "The last time I saw anything that ugly, it had a hook in its mouth."

Oscar Wilde: "Some cause happiness wherever they go; others, whenever they go."

Will Rogers: "She was so ugly she could make a mule back away from an oat bin."

Irvin S. Cobb: "I've just learned about his illness. Let's hope it's nothing trivial."

Clarence Darrow: "I have never killed a man, but I have read many obituaries with great pleasure."

Walter Kerr: "He had delusions of adequacy."

Winston Churchill

A member of Parliament asked Winston Churchill: "Mr. Churchill, must you fall asleep while I'm speaking?"

Churchill replied: "No. It's purely voluntary."

George Bernard Shaw vs Winston Churchill

Shaw sent an invitation to Winston Churchill. It read: "I am enclosing two tickets to the first night of my new play; bring a friend... if you have one."

Churchill replied: "Cannot possibly attend first night, will attend second... if there is one."

Celebrity quotes

Jack Nicholson

"With my sunglasses on, I'm Jack Nicholson: without them, I'm fat and seventy."

Tommy Smothers

"Red meat is not bad for you. Blue green meat is bad for you."

Muhammed Ali on speed

"I'm so fast I can turn out the bedroom light and be in bed before the room gets dark."

Cary Grant

"Everybody wants to be Cary Grant. Even I want to be Cary Grant."

Billy Connolly

"My definition of an intellectual is someone who can listen to the William Tell Overture without thinking of the Lone Ranger."

Dimitri Martin

"The absolute worst time to have a heart attack would have to be... during a game of charades."

Miss Piggy

"Never eat more than you can lift."

Rodney Dangerfield

* The other night I came home and figured I'd play it cool... you know, let my wife make the first move. She went to Florida!

* My wife and I have a terrible relationship. The other day she told me that if I really loved her, I never would have married her.

*I asked my wife if I should be buried or cremated. She said, "Play it safe. Do both."

* I went to see my doctor. I told him, "Doctor every morning when I get up and I look in the mirror, I feel like throwing up. What's wrong with me?"

He said, "I don't know but your eyesight is perfect."

* I have bad luck with doctors. I don't get no respect. You know my doctor don't ya? Doctor Vinnie Boombatz. I called him one night and told him I'd accidentally swallowed a bottle of sleeping pills. He told me to have a few drinks and get some sleep!

* A girl phoned me up and said, "Come on over. There's nobody home." I went over. Nobody was home!

* "This broad was ugly. She was so ugly that if you looked up the word ugly in the dictionary... underneath it you found her picture."

* I come from a long line of very stupid people. My great grandfather was in the civil war. He fought for the west!

* I was feeling really depressed so I called the Suicide Hot-Line! They told me to go for it!

* With my wife I don't get no respect; last night some guy knocked on the front door. She told me to hide in the closet!

* I tell ya, with girls I get no respect. I had a blind date with a girl. I waited two hours at the corner and then a girl showed up.

I asked her, "Are you Louise?"

She asked me, "Are you Rodney?"

When I said, "Yeah," she said, "Well then... I'm not Louise."

Woody Allen

* "The most beautiful words in the English language are not, 'I love you', but... 'It's benign.'"

* "To you I'm an atheist. To God I'm the loyal opposition."

* "There are two types of people in this world; good and bad. The

good people sleep better but that bad people seem to enjoy the waking hours much more."

* "I'm not afraid of death. I just don't want to be there when it happens."

* "Is Knowledge knowable? If not, how do we know that?"

* "You can live to be a hundred if you give up all the things that make you want to live to be a hundred."

* "I don't want to achieve immortality through my work. I want to achieve it through not dying."

* "Eternity is really long. Especially near the end."

* "Most of the time I don't have much fun. The rest of the time, I don't have any fun at all."

* "The lion and the calf shall lie down together but the calf will not get much sleep."

Classics from the TV show Hollywood Squares

Q: "According to Cosmopolitan, if you meet a stranger at a party and you think that he is attractive, is it okay to come out and ask him if he's married?"

Rose Marie: "No… wait until morning."

Q: "Which of your five senses tends to diminish as you get older?"

Charley Weaver: "My sense of decency."

Q: "If you're going to make a parachute jump, at least how high should you be?

Charley Weaver: "Three days of steady drinking should do it."

Q: "According to Ann Landers, is there anything wrong with getting into the habit of kissing a lot of people?"

Charley Weaver: "It got me out of the army."

Q: "Back in the old days, when Great Grandpa put horseradish on his head, what was he trying to do?"

George Gobel: "Get it in his mouth."

Q: "Paul, why do Hell's Angels wear leather?"

Paul Lynde: "Because chiffon wrinkles too easily."

Q: "When you pat a dog on its head he will wag his tail. What will a goose do?"

Paul Lynde: "Make him bark?"

The wit (and wisdom) of sports

Redskins linebacker Joe Jacoby
"I'd run over my own mother to win the Superbowl."

Matt Millen added, "To win one, I'd run over Joe's mom too."

Rocky Graziano
"I quit school in the sixth grade because of pneumonia. Not because I had it, but because I couldn't spell it."

Casey Stengel
"I was such a dangerous hitter I even got intentional walks in batting practice."

Bob Uecker
* "How do you catch a knuckleball? You wait until it stops rolling then go pick it up."
* "I spent three of the best years of my life in 10th grade."
* "I think my top salary was in 1966. I made $17,000 and 11 of that came from selling other players equipment."
* "My usual position in baseball was the player to be named later."
* "I led the league in, 'go get'em next time.'"

Vince Lombardi
"If winning isn't everything, why do they keep score?"

Knute Rockne / Notre Dame
"I've found that prayers work best when you have big players."

John Heisman
"Gentlemen, it is better to have died a small boy than to fumble this football"

Frank Leahy / Notre Dame
"A school without football is in danger of deteriorating into a medieval study hall."

Lou Holtz / Arkansas - Notre Dame
"The man who complains about the way the ball bounces is likely to be the one who dropped it."

Bob Devaney / Nebraska
"I don't expect to win enough games to be put on NCAA

probation. I just want to win enough to warrant an investigation."

Rodney Dangerfield

"I went to a fight the other night and a hockey game broke out!"

Duffy Daugherty / Michigan State

"Football is not a contact sport, it is a collision sport. Dancing is a contact sport."

Darrell Royal / Texas

"Three things can happen when you throw the ball, and two of them are bad."

Bobby Bowden / Florida State

"Son, you've got a good engine, but your hands aren't on the steering wheel."

John McKay/USC

After USC lost 51-0 to Notre Dame, his post-game message to his team was, "All those who need showers… take them."

Boxing trainer Lou Duva

"You can sum up this sport in two words… You never know."

Greg Norman

"I owe a lot to my parents, especially my mother and father."

Pete Rose

"I'd be willing to bet you… if I was betting man, that I have never bet on baseball."

Mike Ditka

"What's the difference between a three week old puppy and a sportswriter? In six weeks the puppy stops whining."

Pat Williams (NBA)

"We can't win at home. We can't win on the road. As general manager, I just can't figure out where else to play."

Gordie Howe)

"All hockey players are bilingual. The know English and profanity."

Wayne Gretzky on fighting in hockey

"Some people ask, 'Are hockey fights real?' I say, 'If they weren't I'd get in more of them.'"

Golf stuff

Dean Martin

If you drink, don't drive… don't even putt.

Bishop Fulton J. Sheen

Man blames fate for all other accidents, but feels personally responsible when he makes a hole-in-one.

Hank Aaron

It took me 17 years to get 3,000 hits in baseball. I did it in one afternoon on the golf course.

David Feherty - CBS golf announcer:

* At Augusta 2011: "It's just a glorious day. The only way to ruin a day like this would be to play golf on it."

* "Watching Phil Mickelson play golf is like watching a drunk chasing a balloon near the edge of a cliff."

* "That ball is so far left, Lassie couldn't find it if it was wrapped in bacon."

Gardner Dickinson

They say golf is like life, but don't believe them. Golf is much more complicated than that.

Billy Graham

The only time my prayers aren't answered is when I'm playing golf.

Jack Lemon

If you think it's hard to meet new people, try picking up the wrong golf ball.

Lee Trevino

* Golf is a game invented by the same people who think music comes out of a bagpipe.

* When I'm on a golf course and it starts to rain and lightning, I hold up my one iron because I know even God can't hit a one-iron."

Did you ever notice that…

No one ever says, "It's only a game" when their team is winning

Two guys are on the putting green

One guy asks the other, "Isn't that a new putter you've got there?"
The other guy says, "Yep."

The first guy asks, "What happened to your old putter?"

The guy replies, "It couldn't swim."

Golfing priorities

One day Phil accidentally overturned his golf cart. Elizabeth, a very attractive and keen golfer, who lived in a villa on the golf course, heard the noise and called out, "Are you okay?"

"I'm okay thanks," Phil replied.

Elizabeth said, "Come on up to my villa, rest a while and I'll help you get the cart up later."

"That's mighty nice of you," he answered, but I don't think my wife would like it."

"Oh, come on," Elizabeth insisted. "I won't tell anybody."

She was very pretty, very sexy, very persuasive and Phil was weak so Phil said, "Okay… but my wife won't like it."

After a few restorative brandys, and some creative putting lessons, Phil told his host: "I feel a lot better now, but I know my wife is going to be really upset so I'd better go."

"Don't be silly Philly," Elizabeth said with a seductive smile, "She won't know anything. By the way, where is she?"

Phil replied, "She's outside under the cart."

Anonymous thoughts about golf

* Did you ever notice that you can hit a 2-acre fairway 10% of the time but you can hit a 2 inch branch 90% of the time.

* A 'gimme' can best be defined as an agreement between two golfers ... neither of whom can putt very well.

* Golf's a hard game to figure. One day you'll go out and slice it and shank it, hit into all the traps and miss every green. The next day you go out and for no reason at all your game really stinks!

* The biggest problem when you're playing golf is that the slow groups are always in front of you and the fast groups are behind you.

* A golf swing improvement will only last three holes.

* The easiest shot in golf is usually your fifth putt.

* A good drive on the 18th hole has stopped many a golfer from giving up the game.

Chapter 2

Legal, political & corporate

J. Paul Getty

"If you owe the bank $100 that's your problem.

If you owe the bank $100 million, that's the bank's problem."

The Golden Rule of business

Them that has the gold... rules.

Business Proverb

When a man says to you, "It isn't the money... it's the principal of the thing." It's the money.

Robin Hall

"Lawyers believe a person is innocent until proven broke."

The importance of being on the same page

A hobo, going door-to-door begging for food, knocked on the door of a well-to-do matron. She replied to his request by telling him that she did not believe in free handouts, but that if he were willing to do some work for her, she would give him some money with which to buy food.

He agreed and she told him, "Behind the house you'll find a bucket of green paint and a brush which you can use to paint the porch."

With a, "Thanks ma'am," he headed for the back of the house.

A few hours later, he knocked on the front door to inform the lady that he had finished the painting.

She gave him fifty dollars for his efforts.

He thanked her and as he turned to leave, he said, "By the way ma'am, that's not a Porsche, it's a Mercedes."

A lawyer's concept of fair play

Two lawyers are in a bank when suddenly, armed robbers burst in. While one of the robbers takes the money from the tellers, the other guy lines the customers– including the lawyers–up against a wall and proceeds to collect their valuables.

As all this is going on, lawyer number one quietly jams something into lawyer number two's hand.

Without looking down, lawyer number two whispers to lawyer number one, "What the heck is this?"

Lawyer number one replies, "It's that $100 I owe you."

The trouble with lawyer jokes

Lawyers don't think they're funny and nobody else thinks they are jokes.

Dick the Butcher to Jack Cade in Shakespeare's Henry IV

"The first thing we do, let's kill all the lawyers."

A client's justice

A lawyer returns to his parked BMW to find the headlights broken and considerable damage to the front end. There is no sign of the offending vehicle but he's relieved to see that there is a note stuck under the windshield wiper.

The note reads: "Sorry. I just backed into your beautiful new Beemer. The witnesses who saw the accident are standing here nodding and smiling at me because they think I'm doing the right thing and leaving my name, address and other particulars which would be helpful to you... but, I'm not!"

What do you call an incompetent lawyer?

A: Your Honor.

What do you call a very incompetent lawyer?

A: Senator.

The difference between a good lawyer and a great lawyer?

A good lawyer knows the law.

A great lawyer knows the judge.

The difference between a good lawyer and a bad lawyer?

A bad lawyer makes your case drag on for years.

A good lawyer makes it last even longer.

Zig Ziglar

"Money isn't the most important thing in life, but it's right up there with oxygen on the 'gotta have it' scale."

Kathleen Norris

"In spite of the high cost of living, it's still very popular."

Wall Street methods explained

Once upon a time, a man came to a village and announced to the villagers that he would buy monkeys for $10 each. Since there were lots of monkeys around, the villagers went out to the forest and started catching them.

The man bought thousands of monkeys at $10 each and then, as the supply started to diminish, the villagers stopped their efforts. In an effort to motivate them, he announced that he would now pay double and buy monkeys at $20 each. So, the freshly motivated villagers went back out and started catching monkeys again.

As the supply diminished even further and people started going back to their farms, the offer increased to $25 each. Ultimately, the supply of monkeys became so diminished that it was a rare thing to even see a monkey, let alone catch it!

The man then announced that he would now buy all monkeys at $50 each however, since he had to go to the city on urgent business, his assistant would buy them on his behalf.

In the man's absence, the assistant said to the villagers, "Look at all these monkeys in the big cage that the man has already collected. I will sell them to you for $35 and when the man returns from the city, you can sell them back to him for $50 each."

So the villagers pooled all their savings, mortgaged their homes and bought all the monkeys for 700 billion dollars.

They never saw the man or his assistant again, only monkeys... lots and lots of monkeys!

Business Q & A

Q: What did the college graduate say to the construction worker?
A: Would you like fries with that sir?

Q: What is the difference between a car salesman and a computer salesman?
A: The car salesman probably knows how to drive a car.

Q: How many union guys does it take to change a lightbulb?
A: Five. You got a frickin' problem with that?

Brian Keelan

"What's the point in being happy if you're broke?"

George Carlin

"Most people work just hard enough not to get fired and get paid just enough money not to quit."

Getting our money's worth

According to the latest government survey, three out of four people make up almost 75% of the population.

The difference between philosophy and religion

Philosophy has questions that may never be answered.

Religion has answers that may never be questioned

Keeping it simple: the one watch theory

A man with one watch knows what time it is but a man with two watches never really knows for sure.

Why salesmen hate sales managers

A sales manager complains to his secretary. "That Fred is so forgetful. I'm amazed that he can sell anything. I asked him to pick me up some sandwiches on his way back from lunch, and I'll bet you five bucks he forgets."

Just then the door flew open, and in bounced Fred. "You'll never guess what happened!" he shouted. "While I was at lunch, I met Old Man Gordon, who hasn't bought anything from us for five years. Well, we got to talking about a few things. We hit it off, one thing led to another and he gave me this huge order for half a million dollars!"

The sales manager turned to his secretary. "See. I told you he'd forget the sandwiches."

The scorpion and the frog

A scorpion and a frog were fleeing a forest fire when they came to a river. The frog immediately jumped in and started to swim across. The scorpion yelled after him, "Hey. Mr. Frog there. You're not going to just swim away and leave me here to die are you?"

The frog turned around and looked back at the scorpion and said, "Well there's not really much else I can do is there?"

The scorpion said, "Hey man… please don't leave me here. I can't swim. Just let me get on your back and since you can swim, you can take me across the river to safety"

The frog said, "What do you think I am? Some kind of a schmuck? As soon as I got you to the other side you'd kill me with that poison stinger of yours. There's no way I'm leaving myself open to that!"

The scorpion said, "I most certainly would not! You would have just saved my life and I would be most grateful to you. There's no way I'd do that. Come on man. I'd do it for you… please."

So the frog, being your basic charitable guy with a heart of gold, let the scorpion get on his back and together, they swam across the river to safety. Just as they got to the other side, the scorpion let go with his stinger and injected a lethal load right into the frogs back.

The poor frog couldn't believe what had happened especially since he had just saved the scorpion's life. He looked at him and with his dying breath he asked the scorpion, "Why did you do that?"

The scorpion replied, "Because I'm a scorpion stupid."

Entrepreneurialism explained

Johnny goes to his dad and asks him for $300 to buy a BMX bike.

His father says, "So you just expect me to give you $300 to buy a bike? Just like that?"

Johnny says, "Well... could you Dad? Please!"

"Well I could son… but I'm not going to."

"Why not dad?"

"Because life just doesn't work like that Johnny. You don't just want something and then somebody gives you the money to buy it."

"Well, how else am I going to get the money for the bike Dad?"

The father, sensing that this would be a great teaching moment said, "Well son, what you need to do here is learn how to think like a businessman… you know… develop your entrepreneurial spirit and come up with a way to earn the money you need. A good creative business idea like say… sell something to somebody for a profit and use the money you make to buy the bike. That's the way it's done in the real world. That's how you get the things you want out of life. Do you understand Johnny?"

"Yes I do Dad and thanks for explaining it to me so well."

A week later the father comes home from work and notices a brand new, tricked out BMX bike in the backyard. He looks at Johnny and asks him, "Where'd you get the cool-looking bike son?"

Johnny very proudly tells him, "Well dad, I took your advice. I sold something for a nice profit and then took the money I made and used it to buy the bike."

Impressed, the father says, "Really. That's great. What did you sell?"

With a huge grin, Johnny replies, "Your boat."

Why CEO's aren't worth the money

On his inaugural tour of the facilities, the new CEO noticed a guy leaning idly against a wall. The room was full of workers and wanting to send a message to show them he meant business, he went over and asked the guy, "How much money do you make a week?"

Caught by surprise, the young man looked at him and said, "I make four hundred dollars a week. Why?"

The CEO smiled at him and said, "Just wait right here."

He went back to his office and returned a few minutes later, went up to the guy and handed him sixteen hundred dollars in cash, telling him as he did so, "Here's four weeks pay. Now get the hell out of here and don't ever come back."

Feeling pretty good about himself, having sent the message and all, the CEO looked around the room and asked, "Does anyone want to tell me what that clown did around here anyway?"

With a chuckle, a voice in the crowd replied, "He was the pizza delivery guy."

A nightmare comes true

A man decides to take a day off and play golf instead of going to work. Just as he is getting ready to putt on the twelfth green, he gets a cell phone call from his boss.

His boss asks, "Is everything okay at the office?"

The nervous hooky player replied, "Yes chief. It's all under control. It's been a very busy day, I haven't stopped once."

"Excellent. In that case maybe you could do me a favor?"

"Of course sir, what is it?"

"Speed it up a little will you. I'm in the foursome behind you."

Lily Tomlin

"The trouble with the rat-race is that even if you win… you're still a rat."

Thinking about a career? Consider this...

"Right now, this is a job. If I advance any higher, this would be my career. And if this were my career, I'd have to throw myself in front of a train." *Jim Halpert: The Office*

W.C. Fields

"Start off each day with a smile and get it over with."

The ultimate Yuppie

The Yuppie had just bought his first BMW and was in a big rush to show it off to his friends so, off he goes... proudly motoring up the main drag. He carefully parked in front of his friend's condo but, in his excitement, he forgot to look when he opened the car door. A taxi sideswiped his car; neatly shearing off the door–along with the guy's arm.

The yuppie, seeing the damage to his pride and joy, jumps out of his car and starts screaming, "My BMW! My beautiful BMW!"

The taxi driver stops, hops out of his car and runs back to the scene in order to try and help the injured yuppie.

He tells him, "Listen man, you are in a state of shock. Your left arm was taken off and you're losing a lot of blood."

The yuppie looks down and seeing that his left arm is gone, starts to yell, "My Rolex! My Rolex is gone!"

The CEO and his son-in-law

A very successful businessman with a rather plain-looking daughter was quite relieved when she finally met a young man and married him.

After they returned from their honeymoon, he had a meeting with his new son-in-law and told him, "I love my daughter very much and now I want to welcome you into the family. To show you how much we care for you, I'm making you a fifty percent partner in my business. All you have to do is come to the factory every day and learn the operation."

The son-in-law interrupted, "Oh I couldn't do that. I hate factories. I can't stand all the noise."

"I see," replied the father-in-law. "Well, then you can work in the office and take over the administration of the business."

"No way! I hate office work," said the son-in-law. "I can't imagine anything worse than being stuck behind a desk."

A little exasperated, the father-in law said, "Now wait just a minute here. I just made you half owner of a large, money-making operation, but you don't like factories and you won't work in an office. What do you suggest I do with you?"

"Simple," said the son-in-law. "Buy me out."

The wit and wisdom of Al Capone

* Slogan for the 1927 Chicago mayoral election: "Vote early and vote often."

* Capone's theory of motivation: "You can get more done with a kind word and a gun than you can with just a kind word."

Why CEO's need their minions

As a young engineer is leaving the office for the day, he finds the Chief Executive Officer standing in front of a shredder with a piece of paper in his hand.

"Listen," said the CEO, "this is a very sensitive and important document, and my secretary is not here. Can you make this thing work?"

"Certainly," said the young engineer.

He turned on the machine, inserted the paper, and pressed the start button.

"There you go sir," he said.

"Excellent, excellent!" said the CEO as his paper disappeared inside the machine, "I just need one copy."

How to sell life insurance

Private Jones was assigned to the Army induction center, where he was given the assignment of advising new recruits about their government benefits, especially their Serviceman's Group Life Insurance (SGLI).

A few months later, the center's Lieutenant noticed that Private Jones had almost a 100% closing record for insurance sales. This had never happened before. Rather than ask about this, the Lieutenant decided to attend one of Private Jones' sales sessions. Standing in the back of the room, he listens to Jones 'pitch' the new recruits.

Jones gave a thorough explanation of the SGLI program and concluded his sales presentation by telling the new recruits, "Now think very carefully about this. If you have the SGLI and are killed in battle, the government has to pay $200,000 to your beneficiaries. But, if you don't have SGLI, and you get killed in battle, the government only has to pay a maximum of $6,000."

After pausing to let the numbers sink in, he concluded, "Now then… which group of soldiers do you think they are going to send into battle first?"

Will Rogers

* "Advertising is the art of convincing people to spend money they don't have for something they don't need."

* "If advertisers spent the same amount of money on improving their products as they do on advertising, they wouldn't have to advertise them."

Legal fees

In the process of shopping for a divorce lawyer, a man goes to a lawyer's office and tells him, "I'm getting a divorce and I wanted to ask you how much you would charge me for legal advice."

The lawyer replied, "I charge $300 for three questions."

The prospective client replied, "$300 for three questions! Don't you think that's kind of expensive?"

The lawyer smiled as he leaned across the desk and said, "Yes, I do. Now what's your third question?"

The Jewish global financial crisis

A Jewish businessman was in a great deal of financial trouble: his business was failing and he had put every dollar he had into the business along with every dollar he could borrow. He owed everybody and was now seriously contemplating suicide.

As a last resort, he went to a Rabbi and tearfully poured out his sad story.

When he had finished, the Rabbi told him, "Here's what I want you should do. Put a beach chair and your Bible in your car and drive down to the beach. Take the beach chair and the Bible to the water's edge, sit down in the beach chair, and put the Bible in your lap.

Next, I want you should open the Bible. The wind will riffle the pages, but eventually the open Bible will come to rest on a page. Now look down at the page and read the first thing you see. Those words will be your answer and point you in the right direction. Then you will know what you need to do next."

A year later the businessman went back to the Rabbi and brought his wife and children with him. The man wore a new custom-tailored suit, his wife wore a beautiful mink coat and the children were well dressed and glowing with happiness. The businessman pulled an envelope stuffed with money out of his pocket, gave it to the Rabbi as a donation and thanked him for his wise advice.

The Rabbi recognized the benefactor, and was very curious as he asked, "You did as I suggested?"

"Right to the letter," replied the businessman.

"You went to the beach?"

"Right to the water's edge."

"You sat in a beach chair with the Bible in your lap?"

"Absolutely."

"You let the wind riffle the pages until they stopped?"

"Just exactly the way you told me to."

"And what were the first words you saw?"

Beaming with pleasure, he said, "Chapter 11!"

The L.A. real estate broker joke

A real estate salesman in Los Angeles who had been working on the sale of a Beverley Hills mansion, called his client one morning, "Good morning Phil. It's Steve here with some good news for you but... there's some bad news too."

Phil replied, "Okay. Give me the good news first."

"You know that house you want to buy over on Sunset Boulevard?"

"Yeah."

"I talked them down a hundred and fifty grand to an even million."

"Way to go Steve. That's great. So then... what's the bad news?"

"Well... the bad news is... they want five hundred dollars down."

George Burns' sales advice

"Sincerity is everything. If you can fake that, you've got it made."

The difference between war and revolution

War is when the government tells you who the bad guy is.

Revolution is when you decide that for yourself.

The difference between mechanical and civil engineers

Mechanical engineers build weapons.

Civil engineers build targets.

The best 2008 global financial crisis quote

"This is much worse than a divorce... I've lost over half of my net worth and I still have my wife!"

Best lawyer joke # 1

A lawyer calls home from his office one morning and when a strange voice answers the phone, he says, "Hi, you must be the new maid."

"Uh... yes I am," came the reply.

"Well then, welcome aboard. Now then, would you please be so kind as to put my wife on the phone for me?"

The new maid hesitatingly replied, "Well sir, I'm sorry, but she uh... she can't come to the phone right now."

The lawyer asks, "Why not?"

"Well sir, she's ...ahhhhh...she's upstairs and uhhh.... she's... aahhhh... in the bedroom and she's... uhhhh ...."

With an air of impatience, he says, "Come on. Come on... out with it. What is she doing?"

"Well, she's uhhh... she's uhhhhh... uhhh... she's upstairs in the bedroom and she's fooling around with the mailman."

Outraged by what he has just heard, the lawyer replied, "Oh, she is, is she?"

He pauses for a moment to think and then says, "Well here's what I'd like you to do. Go into the den and look in the lower right hand drawer of the desk where you'll find a 45 automatic pistol. Be careful now... it's loaded.

Now then, once you have the gun, I want you to take it and very quietly go upstairs and shoot them both in the head. Don't worry about any trouble. I'm a big-time lawyer and I'll get you off in no time at all. I'll also reward you very handsomely."

"Okay," she said and laid the phone down.

A few minutes later, the lawyer hears a couple of gunshots in the background.

Shortly thereafter, the maid comes back on the phone and tells him, "Okay... I did it."

"Good," says the lawyer. "Now here's what I want you to do next. I want you to go back upstairs and drag of the bodies out into the backyard. Then I want you to throw them both into the swimming pool."

The maid replies, "The swimming pool! What swimming pool?"

This was followed by a very pregnant pause... and then the lawyer asked, "Hey, wait a second, is this 542-7157?"

Best lawyer joke # 2

A young lawyer in Hollywood is trying to make his mark as a theatrical agent. Unfortunately, he is not doing very well; he can't get any good clients and he can't make any deals.

Late one night, he is sitting in his office wondering just what has gone so wrong. There is a loaded gun lying on the desk in front of him along with a bottle of whiskey and he is seriously contemplating ending it all.

Suddenly there is a puff of smoke and, lo and behold, standing before him–pitchfork and all–is the devil himself.

The devil tells him, "Look, I know you're doing lousy in this business and you're thinking about ending it all, so before you do anything that you might regret later, I am prepared to make you a very substantial offer. Are you interested?"

"Keep going," the agent replied.

"As of tomorrow morning, you will be the exclusive agent for life, for George Clooney, Brad Pitt, Adam Sandler, Kanye West and Angelina Jolie. However... in return for this opportunity I am offering you, your wife will die, your children will die and their souls will burn in Hell for all eternity."

The lawyer/agent slowly raised his head, arched one eyebrow and looked at him with a very suspicious grin.

Smiling now, he asked, "So... what's the catch?"

Dan Quayle for president?

Former Vice President, Dan Quayle and his wife are spending a quiet evening at home. Dan is reading a comic book and Mrs Quayle is writing a letter.

She pauses and asks, "Dan, how do you spell Mississippi?"

Dan slowly looks up from his task, poses thoughtfully, and thinks for a moment. After all, he who once said that, "Verbosity leads to inarticulate things," wanted to be clear on exactly what she wanted in an effort to avoid being verbose or inarticulate or even worse… both.

He asked her, "What do you want, the State or the river?"

The regal Ronald Reagan

Queen Elizabeth and Prince Philip were visiting President Reagan at his California ranch. Over dinner Reagan learned that Queen Elizabeth was an ardent horse lover and an accomplished equestrian. Ever the complete host, Reagan told the Queen that he had arranged a morning ride for them – English saddles and all.

The Queen was delighted by this. The next morning, they mounted their English-saddled horses and headed out.

Just as they got outside the corral, Queen Elizabeth's horse let go with a tremendously loud fart. This wasn't just passing a little gas… this occurred at a volume that was impossible to ignore.

The Queen reigned in as she blushed a deep shade of crimson and turned to Reagan, saying, "Oh dear, I am so embarrassed."

The ever gallant Reagan replied, "Oh please don't be embarrassed, Your Highness. It's perfectly natural. Heck… I thought it was your horse."

Bill Clinton learns the brutal truth

While President and Mrs. Clinton were on vacation in Arkansas, they took a few days off for themselves and went on a car trip. Along the way, they stopped at a service station to fill up and it turned out that the owner of the station was Hillary's first high school love. They talked for a few minutes, exchanged a few reminiscences and then the Clintons paid their bill and continued on their way.

As they were driving away, Bill put his arm around Hillary and said, "Now y'a see, honey, it's a good thing you married me because if you had married that man, then today, you would be the wife of a service station owner."

She looked at him, smiled sweetly and replied, "Wrong again Billy boy. If I had married that man, then today he would be the President of the United States."

A Canadian Prime Minister learns from a US President

Back in the day, Canadian Prime Minister Brian Mulroney was visiting US President Ronald Reagan in Washington. During a moment alone in the oval office, Reagan asked Mulroney, "So Brian, how are you doing as far as handling and controlling your minions?"

"I don't believe I understand what you mean Ronnie," said Brian.

"Just a second and I'll show you," said Reagan as he picked up the phone. He barked into the phone, "Bush, you incompetent dork. Get your ass in here! On the double!"

Promptly, Bush came running into the office, "Yes, Mr. President. What can I do for you?"

"Bush, I've got a little question for you. Your mother has a kid but it's not your brother and it's not your sister. Who is it?"

Bush thought real hard for a moment then said, "Give me a couple of minutes to work it out and I'll get right back to you."

"OK, but make it snappy!" said Reagan.

Bush left only to return a few minutes later saying, "I have the answer Sir. It's me!"

"That's right, now get the hell out of here and get back to work."

"Yessir, Mr. President," Bush replied and left.

Reagan turned to Mulroney and said, "See what I mean Brian? You've got to let these guys know who's in charge. Keep'em on their toes."

"Yes I most certainly do Ronnie. Thanks for the tip. I'll give it a shot when I get back to Canada."

About two weeks later, Mulroney is in his office in Ottawa and he decides to try out Reagan's idea. He picks up his phone and barks, "Clarke! Get your skinny butt in here!"

A few minutes later, an out of breath Joe Clarke comes running into the office. "Yes Mr. Prime Minister. What can I do for you?" he asks.

"Clarke, I've got a question for you. Suppose your mother has a kid. It's not your brother and it's not your sister. Who is it?"

Clarke ponders this for a few seconds, then says, "Just give me a few minutes to work out the answer and I'll get right back to you."

"Alright," says Mulroney, "But hurry up!"

As Clarke runs down the hallway, he bumps into Finance minister

Michael Wilson.

"Michael," he says. "I've got a question for you. Your mother has a kid but it's not your brother and it's not your sister. Have you got any idea who that might be?"

"Oh, that's easy," says Wilson, "It's me!"

With a look like all the lights just came on, Clark replied, "Right. That's it! Okay... thanks Mike."

He hurries back to Mulroney's office, bursts in and proudly announces, "I've got the answer!"

"Who is it?" asks Mulroney.

"It's Michael Wilson," Clarke replies.

Mulroney stands up yelling, "Wrong again you incompetent dork! It's George Bush!"

George Bush learns to count

Donald Rumsfeld was giving President Bush his daily briefing and he concluded by saying, "And yesterday, Mr. President, three Brazilian soldiers were killed."

"Oh no!" the president exclaimed. "That's terrible!"

The presidential staff was stunned at this display of emotion. They stood nervously watching as the president sat there moaning and sobbing with his head in his hands.

Finally, he looked up and asked, "Donald... just exactly how many is a brazillion?"

Lawyers vs engineers

Three lawyers and three engineers are traveling by train to a conference. At the station ticket counter, the three lawyers each buy a ticket and are surprised to see that the three engineers buy only a single ticket.

"How are three people going to travel on only one ticket?" asked one of the three lawyers.

"Watch and you'll see," answered one of the engineers.

They all board the train. The lawyers take their respective seats but all three engineers cram into a restroom and close the door behind them. Shortly after the train has departed, the conductor comes around collecting tickets.

He knocks on the restroom door and says, "Ticket, please."

The door opens just a crack and a single arm emerges with a ticket in hand. The conductor takes it and moves on.

The lawyers saw this and agreed it was quite a clever idea and after the conference, they decided to copy the engineers on the return trip and save some money.

When they get to the station, the lawyers buy a single ticket for the return trip but to their astonishment, they notice that the engineers don't even buy a ticket.

"How are you going to travel without a ticket?" asks one perplexed lawyer.

"Watch and you'll see," says one of the engineers.

When they board the train, the three engineers cram into a restroom and the three lawyers cram into another one nearby.

Shortly after the train departs, one of the engineers leaves his restroom and walks over to the restroom where the lawyers are hiding. He knocks on the door and says, "Ticket please."

Murderers logic

A man is on trial for murdering his wife after he caught her fooling around with their neighbour. When the prosecuting attorney asked why he shot her instead of the guy she was fooling around with he replied, "I figured it was better to shoot her once instead of shooting a different guy every week."

Government Verbosity

This is what happens when you let the politicians do it:

Pythagorean theorem: 24 words.

The Lord's Prayer: 66 words.

Archimedes' Principle: 67 words.

The Ten Commandments: 179 words.

Gettysburg address: 286 words.

Declaration of Independence: 1,300 words.

U.S. Govt. regulations on cabbage sales: 26,911 words.

Legal pretenses

A young lawyer had just started his own firm. He rented a beautiful office and furnished it lavishly. On opening day–sitting there at his new desk–he saw a man enter the outer office. Wishing to appear as the busy, hot-shot legal beagle, he picked up the phone and started to pretend he had a big deal working. He threw huge figures around and really played the role to a tee.

Finally he hung up and asked the visitor, "Can I help you?"

The man said, "Yeah, I'm here to hook up your phone lines."

Mitt Romney's favorite joke

A Vatican Cardinal burst into the Pope's office one morning in hysterics. "Your Holiness, I have astounding news but it's both good and bad. Jesus has returned. He's on the phone. He wants to talk to you!"

The Pope jumps up and says, "The second coming. That's great! But what could possibly be bad news after great news like that?"

The Cardinal replies, "He's calling from Salt Lake City!"

Blondes and business don't mix

A blonde is in Wal-Mart with her new cell phone; a gift from her husband.

Her phone rings and it's her husband who asks, "How do you like your new cell phone sweetie?"

She says, "Oh it's just great honey, I love it. But… how did you know I was at Wal-mart?"

The need to feel something good

A guy walks into a shoe store and asks for a pair of shoes: size eight. The obviously well trained salesman says, "But sir, you take at least an eleven; maybe even an eleven-and-a-half."

"Just bring me a size eight!" the man replies.

The sales guy brings them and the man stuffs his feet into them. Then he stands up in obvious pain, turns to the salesman and says, "I've just lost my house to the I.R.S. and I live with my mother-in-law. My eighteen year old daughter ran off with my best friend and my business has just filed for Chapter 11. The only thing I can look forward to is to come home at night and take my shoes off."

The value of knowing who your real competition is

Two guys are camping in the mountains of British Columbia. One of the guys is resting in their tent one morning when the other guy comes running into the tent at top speed. He sits down and quickly starts lacing on his running shoes.

The guy in bed says, "Hey Joe! What the heck is going on?"

Joe replies, "Jesus man! The biggest, meanest grizzly bear in the world is running down the mountain, headed straight for us. He's real pissed off and he's going to kill us and then eat us!"

"So what are you bothering with the running shoes for Joe? You can't outrun a grizzly bear."

Joe replies, "I don't have to outrun him. I just have to outrun you!"

A New York moment

A New Yorker is forced to take a day off from work to go to court after being ticketed for an improper left turn. After sitting all day in court waiting for his number to come up his case is finally called at 2:30 p.m. He is then informed that court would be adjourned until the next day and he would have to take another day off work for this matter.

"What for?" he yelled at the judge.

The judge was a little short of temper at this point, since he was a bit of a self-important stuffed shirt anyway and did not like having his authority questioned. He slammed his gavel down and retorted, "Fifty dollars for contempt of court, that's what for!"

With a pained expression, the man pulled out his wallet and started counting his cash.

As he watched him do that, the judge had an uncharacteristic turn of heart and said, "That's OK. You don't have to pay the fine right now."

The man replied, "Oh that's not the problem your honor. I'm just checking to see if I have enough for two more words."

Definitions:

A jury: 12 people whose job it is to determine which client has the better attorney.

An accountant: A guy who marries Jennifer Lopez for her money.

An economist: A guy who will know tomorrow why the things he predicted yesterday didn't happen today.

An auditor: A guy who comes onto the battlefield after the battle and shoots the survivors.

A consultant: Someone who takes the watch off your wrist and then tells you the time.

Stress:

* When you wake up screaming and you realize you weren't asleep.

* That feeling that arises when you are frantically trying to suppress the urge to beat the living daylights out of some dickhead who desperately needs it.

A programmer: A guy who solves a problem you didn't know you had in a way that you don't understand.

A diplomat: A guy who can tell you to go hell in way that will have you looking forward to the trip.

Political correctness: A doctrine, fostered by a delusional, illogical minority which holds forth the proposition that it is entirely possible to pick up a turd by the clean end.

And just so you'll know…

Q: What's the difference between a micro-economist and a macro-economist?

A: Micro-economists are wrong about specific things while macro-economists are wrong about things in general.

The difference between a tax and a fine

A fine is a tax for doing wrong. A tax is a fine for doing well.

Murphy's laws

Murphy's original law: Whatever can go wrong, will go wrong … and at the worst possible time.

"Murphy" was Ed Murphy, an engineer in the 1940s working on experiments involving the rocket sled.

One day Murphy commented about a technician who had mis-wired some equipment, that "if there's any way to do things wrong, he will." And it caught on.

50-50-90 Rule: Anytime you have a 50-50 chance of getting something right, there's a 90% probability you'll get it wrong.

The rule of gardening: When weeding, the best way to make sure you are removing a weed and not a valuable plant is to pull on it. If it comes out of the ground easily, it was a valuable plant.

Law of life: The light at the end of the tunnel is usually a train.

Law of things lost: The easiest way to find something lost around the house is to buy a replacement.

Law of hardness: The hardness of the butter is inversely proportional to the softness of the bread.

Law of Probability: The probability of being watched is directly proportional to the stupidity of your act.

Law of Close Encounters: The probability of meeting someone you know increases dramatically when you are with someone you don't want to be seen with.

Law of Random Numbers: If you dial a wrong number, you never get a busy signal and someone always answers.

Law of Probable Dispersal: Whatever hits the fan will not be evenly distributed.

Law of banking: In order to get a loan you must be able to prove to the bank that you don't need the money.

Law of the Result: When you try to prove to someone that a machine won't work, it will!

Law of Priorities: If you and a tiger are starving to death… the tiger will be the last to die.

Law of trust: Trust only those who stand to lose as much or more than you when things for wrong.

Law of Progress reports: The length of a progress report is inversely proportional to the amount of progress achieved.

Law of damages: If there is a possibility of several things going wrong, the one that causes the most damage will always be the one that goes wrong

Law of the future: The further away the future is, the better it looks.

Law of errors: To err is human. To blame it on somebody else is even more human.

Law of feasibility studies: The more money spent on a feasibility study, the more feasible the project will be.

Law of the will: Where there's a will, there's a won't.

Law of Returns: You get the most of what you need the least.

Law of the shit storm: The speed at which a woman replies, "nothing" when asked, "what's wrong sweetheart?" is inversely proportional to the size and severity of the shit storm that is coming your way.

Guess who said this?

"The budget should be balanced, the Treasury should be refilled, public debt should be reduced, the arrogance of officialdom should be tempered and controlled, and the assistance to foreign lands should be curtailed lest Rome become bankrupt.

People must again learn to work, instead of living on public assistance."

* The answer awaits you at the very end of this chapter.

Great ad slogans

* At a Chicago radiator shop: "Best place in town to take a leak."
* On a plastic Surgeon's door: "Hello. Can we pick your nose?"
* On a plumber's truck: "We repair what your husband fixed."
* On an electrician's truck: "Let us remove your shorts."
* At a propane filling station: "Tank heaven for little grills."
* On a Pizza Shop: "7 days without pizza makes one weak."

What are we doing here?

Most people who live in the city came there from the country in order to make enough money so they could retire and move back to the country.

Ignorance or apathy

After an election, one of the newly elected officials was asked by a reporter what he thought was the cause of such low voter turnout... ignorance or apathy?

"Frankly," the happy winner declared, "I don't know... and I don't care."

The theory of economists

One night a policeman saw a macroeconomist looking for something underneath a light pole and asked him if he had had lost something there.

The economist said, "No. I lost my keys over in the alley."

The policeman asked him why he was looking by the light pole.

The economist responded, "It's a lot easier to look over here."

Why did God create economists?

A: To make weather forecasters look good.

Political & Economic thoughts

Woody Allen

"More than any time in history mankind faces a crossroads. One path leads to despair and utter hopelessness, the other to total extinction. Let us pray that we have the wisdom to choose correctly."

Will Rogers

"Communism is like prohibition: it's a good idea but it won't work."

James Bovard

"Democracy must be something more than two wolves and a sheep voting on what to have for dinner."

David Letterman

"George Bush is writing a book. It's all part of his war on literacy."

Red Adair

"If you think it's expensive to hire a professional to do the job, wait until you hire an amateur."

Golda Meir

"Moses dragged us for 40 years through the desert to bring us to the one place where there was no oil."

W. H. Auden

"We are here on earth to do good unto others. What the others are here for I have no idea."

Douglas Casey

"Foreign aid is the transfer of money from poor people in rich countries to rich people in poor countries."

Margaret Thatcher

"The real problem with socialism is that you eventually run out of other people's money."

Oscar Ameringer

"Politics is the art of getting votes from the poor and campaign funds from the rich, by promising to protect each from the other."

Nikita Khrushchev

"Politicians are the same all over. They promise to build a bridge even where there is no river."

Dan Quayle

"We are ready for any unforeseen event that may or may not occur."

Gordon Liddy

"A liberal is someone who feels a great debt to his fellow man, which debt he proposes to pay off with your money."

Texas Guinan

"A politician is a guy who will lay down your life for his country."

Marty Allen

"A study of economics usually reveals that the best time to buy anything is last year."

George Bernard Shaw

"A government which robs Peter to pay Paul can always depend on the support of Paul."

Darren Weinberg

"It doesn't matter whether you win or lose. The only thing that matters is whether or not I win or lose."

Joseph Stalin

"The people who vote decide nothing. The people who count the votes decide everything."

Fran Lebowitz

"In the Soviet Union, capitalism triumphed over communism. In this country, capitalism triumphed over democracy."

David Frost

"This is what has to be remembered about the law; beneath that cold, harsh, impersonal exterior beats a cold, harsh, impersonal heart."

Fred Allen

"I learned law so well, the day I graduated I sued the college, won the case, and got my tuition back."

President Franklin Roosevelt

"A conservative is a man with two perfectly good legs who has never learned to walk forward."

Stephen Wright - in defense of lawyers

"Ninety nine percent of all lawyers give the rest a bad name."

Ronald Reagan

"When you are up to your armpit in alligators, it's tough to remember that your initial objective was to drain the swamp."

Winston Churchill

* "The inherent vice of capitalism is the unequal sharing of blessings; the inherent virtue of socialism is the equal sharing of miseries."

 * "For a nation to try to tax itself into prosperity is like a man standing in a bucket and trying to lift himself up by the handle."

* "Lawyers occasionally stumble over the truth, but most of them pick themselves up and hurry off as if nothing had happened."

* A lie can get halfway around the world before the truth can even get its pants on."

Political bickering

"Watching the Republicans and the Democrats bicker over the U.S. debt is like watching two drunks argue over a bar bill on the Titanic."

Groucho Marx

 "Politics is the art of looking for trouble, finding it everywhere, diagnosing it incorrectly and applying the wrong remedies."

W.C. Fields

* "Horse sense is the thing a horse has which keeps it from betting on people."

* "Remember, a dead fish can swim downstream but it takes a live one to swim upstream."

* "If you can't dazzle'em with your dancing, then you just baffle them with your bullshit."

Brian Keelan

Sell a man a fish and you feed him for a day. Teach him how to fish and you have just ruined a fantastic business opportunity.

Answer to "Guess who said this?"

Cicero said that and he said it in 54 B.C.

Chapter 3

Fast thinkers

The fast thinking grocer

Fergus was a thrifty old guy who absolutely abhorred the idea of wasting money. One morning he approached the produce manager of his local grocery store and asked him, "How much would ye be chargin' me for a half a head o'lettuce?"

The produce manager politely replied, "I'm sorry sir, we only sell lettuce by the whole head."

A little steamed by this, Fergus replied, "What are ye laddie? Deaf or somethin'? It's a half a head o' lettuce I'm needin' and it's a half a head o' lettuce I'll be buyin'! Now tell me exactly how much it is for a half a head of lettuce and be quick about it!"

The produce manager decided not to get into an argument out on the sales floor, so he said, "Excuse me please, I'll have to go and check with the store manager."

That said, he turned and headed for the store manager's office where he told the manager, "I've got some jerk out here who wants to buy a half a head of lettuce."

After saying this, he heard a, "harumpf,' type of noise behind him. He turned around and was shocked to see that old Fergus had followed him... right into the office!

The startled produce manager mustered a nervous smile, turned to face his manager and continued, "And this fine gentleman here, would like to buy the other half."

A fast thinking speeder

A new Shelby Cobra owner was out on the interstate: top down, tunes playing. Everything felt right so he decided to open her up.

Just as the needle jumped up close to 100 mph, he saw a flashing red and blue light behind him. *"I'm in deep doo doo now,"* he thought as he pulled over.

The cop came up to him, took his license without a word, and examined it. Then he told the nervous driver, "Listen mister. I'm just finishing up a really tough shift and this is my last pull-over. I don't feel like doing any more paperwork, so I'll make you a deal here: if you can give me an excuse for your speeding that I haven't heard before, I'll let you go!"

The guy thought for a moment then said, "Okay… here goes… last week my wife ran off with a cop, and I was afraid you were trying to catch me so you could give her back!"

The cop smiled, handed the man his license and said, "That was beautiful man! You're out of here!"

A really fast thinking speeder

A guy gets pulled over for speeding – 88 MPH in a 45 zone. The cop asks for his driver's license and the guy says, "I'm sorry officer, my license was suspended after my 5th DUI."

The cop asks for his registration and the guy says, "It's in the glove compartment, but it's not in my name because I stole this car in a car-jacking. I killed the woman that owns the car and stuffed her body in the trunk. The gun I used is stashed in the glove compartment."

At this point, the cop pulls his gun and tells the guy to keep his hands in sight while he radios for back-up. Twenty minutes later a supervisor shows up and the cop tells him the story. The supervisor approaches the speeder and asks to see his driver's license.

He hands over a perfectly valid and up-to-date license.

Then the supervisor asks for the registration and the guy tells him, "It's in the glove compartment."

The supervisor tells the guy to keep his hands in sight, walks around to the passenger side and opens the glove compartment. There is the registration in the guy's name and everything seems in order.

Next, the supervisor asks the guy to get out and open the trunk. The guy opens the trunk and the only thing in there is a spare tire. At this point, the confused supervisor tells the guy what the other cop had told him.

With a derisive sneer the guy says, "Really? I'll bet you that son-of-a-gun told you I was speeding too!"

The fast thinking medieval guy

A medieval astrologer prophesied to the king that his favorite mistress would soon die. Sure enough, she died a short time later.

The angry king was certain that the astrologer's prophecy had brought about the woman's death so he summoned the astrologer and commanded him: "Okay oh great prophesier of doom, if thou thinkest that thou art the knower of all things, then thou shouldst thence be able to telleth me whenst thou, thine own self, wouldst die!"

The astrologer, figuring that it was the king's intention to kill him, no matter what answer he gave, thought about it for a moment and then replied, "I do not know exactly when it is that I shalt die sire but this I do know sire that whenever I do die... the king will die three days later."

A fast thinking dog owner

Fred answers the door to find a policeman who tells him that there is a complaint from his neighbour who claimed that Fred's dog had chased him as he rode his bike.

"That's impossible!" Fred claimed.

"What makes you say that?" the policeman asked.

Fred replied, "My dog doesn't have a bike."

A fast thinking fisherman meets a fast thinking snake

A Louisiana man went fishing one early morning but when he got out in the lake he realized that he didn't have any worms to use for bait. Just then, he spied a cottonmouth snake with a frog in its mouth swimming along beside his boat. He thought to himself; *"Frogs are good bass bait... even better than worms."*

Figuring that the snake couldn't bite him with the frog in its mouth, he reached down and grabbed the snake right behind the head. Then he carefully worked the frog out of the snake's mouth and put it in the bait bucket.

Now he had a problem; *"How do I release this snake without getting bit?*

In a brilliant burst of fast-thinking, he grabbed his bottle of Jack Daniels and poured a good sized shot right into the snake's mouth. About ten seconds later, the snake's eyes rolled back into its head and its whole body went limp. He then released the snake into the lake and went fishing - using the frog for bait of course.

Ten minutes later the fisherman felt a nudge at his foot and he looked down to see the snake.

This time it had two frogs in its mouth.

The fast thinking naval captain

A Navy captain executed a few fancy and very daring maneuvers with his ship: maneuvers that had never been sanctioned by the powers that be. The fleet admiral was most annoyed by this showoff and sent a short message.

When told by the captain to read the message in front of a bridge full of officers, the radioman was a little nervous and hesitant.

"Read the bloody message and be quick about it!" the captain roared.

The nervous radioman read aloud, "You are the dumbest, most ignorant son-of-a-bitch to ever sail the seven seas!"

"Very good son," the captain replied. "Now take that below and have it decoded."

A very fast thinking fisherman

A Michigan man in a truck was leaving a spot well known for its fishing when he was stopped by a game warden. In the back of his truck, the warden found two ice chests full of water; each one teeming with live, freshly caught fish.

The game warden asked the man, "Do you have a license to catch those fish?"

The man replied, "Officer, I don't need a license. Those are just my pet fish."

The surprised warden said, "Pet fish?"

"Yep. Every night I bring them down to the river and let 'em swim' round for a while. Then I whistle and they jump right back into the ice chest and I take 'em back home."

The warden retorted, "Don't give me any of that crap! Fish can't do that!"

The man looked at the game warden and said, "I'm not kidding you man. It's true. In fact I can even prove it to you."

The skeptical game warden said, "Okay then… show me!!"

The man poured the fish into the river and stood there waiting. After several minutes, the game warden turned to him and said, "Well?"

"Well, what?" said the man.

"When are you going to call them back?"

The man looked at him like he had six heads and asked, "Call who back?"

The warden answered, "The fish!"

The guy smiled and turned to the warden with a quizzical look, "Really? Fish eh?... What fish?"

A rare fast thinking blonde

A lawyer and a blonde are sitting next to each other on a flight from L.A. to New York. The lawyer leans over and asks the blonde if she would like to play a fun game. The blonde just wants to take a nap, so she politely declines and turns toward the window to catch a few winks.

The lawyer persists and explains that the game is really easy and a lot of fun, "I ask you a question, and if you don't know the answer, you pay me five dollars and vice versa."

Again, she politely declines and tries to get some sleep.

The lawyer, now somewhat agitated, says, "Okay, I'll tell you what. If you don't know the answer you pay me five dollars but, if I don't know the answer, I will pay you fifty dollars."

This catches the blonde's attention and, figuring that there will be no end to this torment unless she plays, she agrees to the game. The lawyer asks the first question: "What is the distance from the earth to the moon?"

The blonde doesn't say a word. She just reaches into her purse, pulls out a five-dollar bill and hands it to the lawyer.

Now, it's her turn. She asks the lawyer: "What goes up a hill with three legs, and comes down with four?"

Puzzled, the lawyer takes out his laptop and searches all his references. Then he hooks the laptop to his cell-phone and via the wireless connection to his modem at his office, he searches the Internet and ultimately, the entire Library of Congress. Frustrated, he sends an e-mail to all his co-workers, friends and clients… nothing.

Finally, he wakes the blonde and hands her a fifty dollar bill. She takes the fifty and turns away to go back to sleep.

The lawyer asks, "Well then, what is the answer?"

Without a word, the blonde hands the lawyer five dollars and goes back to sleep.

The fast thinking pastor

There were two rich and powerful, evil brothers who used their wealth and power to conceal their evil ways from the public eye. They even went to the same church in an effort to project the image of being good upright Christians.

One year, the old pastor of their church retired and a new, younger man was hired. He instantly saw through the evil brothers' deception and he spoke the truth about them to his flock. He also started a fund-raising campaign to build a new church and it was during this time that one of the evil brothers died.

The surviving evil brother went to the young pastor and offered him all the money needed to finish the new church. However, the surviving, evil brother did have a rather large string attached to his gift: "I want you to give the eulogy for my brother and in your speech you must say that my brother was a saint."

The pastor thought about that for a moment and then agreed whereupon he accepted and then, deposited the cheque.

The next day at the funeral, the pastor began his eulogy: "He was a very evil man. He cheated on his wife. He abused his friends, his family and all of his business associates. He had no moral or ethical scruples whatsoever....

But... compared to his brother... he was a saint!"

The fast thinking old guy in a doctor's office

An elderly man, who has just moved to a new town takes ill and decides that he needs to see a doctor. In the waiting room at the clinic, he tries to find out a bit about the doctor so he asks the man sitting next to him if the doctor is a specialist. The man replies that the doctor specializes in everything.

The old man thinks about this for a minute and feeling a little apprehensive, he asks if the doctor's fees are expensive.

The man says, "Well, he is and he isn't. You see, he charges you one thousand dollars for your first visit."

The old man looks even more worried now and exclaims in amazement, "A thousand dollars! That's a lot of money!"

The man replies, "Yes it is, but all your visits after that - for the rest of your life - are free!"

The old man thinks about this as he waits and soon he is called by the nurse to go in to see the doctor.

Upon entering the doctor's office, he says casually, "Hello there doctor, here I am again!"

The fast thinking airplane passenger

This guy is on an airplane, sitting next to an older lady who falls asleep shortly after takeoff. When the plane encounters some turbulence, the guy gets an upset stomach and promptly barfs... all over the nice, little old lady sleeping beside him.

A few minutes later, she wakes up and is totally shocked to see the disgusting mess all over her. She turns and glares at the guy beside her who smiles at her and asks, "Feel better now?"

Fast thinking and drinking

Two drivers climb out of their cars after colliding at an intersection. One of them pulls a flask of Scotch from his pocket and offers it to the other guy as he says, "Here, have a nip of this to calm your nerves."

"Thanks," says the other driver who proceeds to take a good, long swig. Then he offers it back to the owner saying, "Here, you have one too."

The flask owner smiles at him and says, "I'll pass. The police are gonna be here soon."

A fast thinking Irish priest

A farmer named Muldoon, lived alone in the countryside with his beloved Golden Lab, 'Mike.' After many long years of good and faithful companionship, poor old Mike finally died. Muldoon, in his grief, went to visit the parish priest.

He told him, "Father, me dear old dog 'Mike' has passed away and I was wonderin' if you could be persuaded to offer a mass for the poor dead creature?"

Father Patrick replied, "Muldoon, I am so very sorry to hear about your poor dog's death but, unfortunately we cannot have services for an animal in the church.

However, there's a new denomination down the road, and there's no telling what those heathens believe. Maybe they'll do something for the poor animal."

Muldoon said, "I want ta thank y'a greatly for your time and consideration of this matter Father. I'll go there right now. Do you think $5,000 would be enough to donate for the service?"

Father Patrick replied, "One thing I forgot to ask you Muldoon. Was your dog a Catholic?"

A faster thinking Irish priest

Father O'Malley answers the phone and a voice asks, "Hello. Is this Father O'Malley?"

Father O'Malley replies, "Indeed it is!"

"This is the Internal Revenue Service. Can you help us?"

"I can!"

"Do you know a Ted Houlihan?"

"I do!"

"Is he a member of your congregation?"

"Indeed he is!"

"Did he donate $10,000 to the church?"

"Indeed he did. In fact I'll be picking up his check this afternoon."

A fast thinking married woman

A recently retired guy and his wife are in bed one night and he tells her, "Sweetheart, if I were to die suddenly, I want you to sell all my stuff immediately."

She asks him, "Now why would you want me to do something like that?"

"Well," he says, "you're a very attractive woman and I know that some other guy would ask you to marry him and I just don't want some jerk using all my stuff."

She smiles and replies, "Sweetheart… what makes you think I'd marry another jerk?"

The fast thinking retired mafioso

A retired Mafia guy who lived alone in New Jersey wanted to plant his annual tomato garden. It was very difficult work, as the ground was hard and his only son, Vincent, who used to help him, was now in prison.

In a brilliant burst of fast-thinking, he wrote a letter to his son describing his predicament:

Dear Vincent,

This is a sad time for me, because it looks like I won't be able to plant my tomato garden this year. I'm just getting too old to be digging up a garden plot.

I know that if you were here my troubles would be over since I know you would be happy to dig the plot for me, like in the old days.

Wishing you were here,

Papa

A few days later he received a letter from his son:

Dear Pop,

Whatever you do, do not dig up that garden! That's where all the bodies are buried!

Love,

Vinnie

At 4 a.m. the next morning, FBI agents along with the local police arrived and dug up the entire area without finding any bodies whereupon they apologized to the old man and left.

That next day the old man received another letter from his son:

Dear Pop,

You can go ahead and plant the tomatoes now. Sorry I'm not there to help but this is the best I could do given the circumstances.

Love,

Vinnie

A faster thinking single woman

Bob was a single guy living at home with his father and working in the family business. When his aging father got very sick, Bob, realizing that he was soon going to inherit a fortune, decided it was time to find a wife with whom to raise a family and share his wealth.

One evening at an investment meeting, he spotted the most beautiful woman he had ever seen. Her natural beauty took his breath away.

He invited her out to dinner and during the course of their evening together, he told her, "I may look like an ordinary guy to you, but in just a few years, my father will die and then I will inherit a business along with an estate worth well over two hundred million dollars."

Impressed, the woman asked for his business card and three days later, she became... his stepmother.

A fast thinking farmer vs. faster thinking kids

A farmer in the country has a watermelon patch and upon inspection, he discovers that some of the local kids have been helping themselves to a feast. In an effort to discourage the kids from eating into his profits, the farmer puts up a sign that reads:

WARNING!

One of these watermelons contains CYANIDE!

The farmer returns a week later to discover that none of the watermelons have been eaten, but he does find another sign that reads: You've got two now pal!

The fast thinking fish salesman

A customer at Marv's Gourmet Grocery marveled at Marv's quick wit and intelligence so one day he asked him, "Tell me Marv, what is it that makes you so smart?"

"I have never shared my secret with anyone," Marv replies and then lowering his voice so the other shoppers won't hear, he continues, "But since you're such a good and faithful customer, I'll let you in on it. It's the fish heads. You eat enough of them and you'll be positively brilliant."

"You sell them here?" the customer asks.

"I certainly do," says Marv, "Only $4 each."

So... the customer buys three.

A week later, he's back in the store complaining that the fish heads were disgusting and he isn't any smarter.

"That's because you didn't eat enough of them," says Marv.

This time the customer gives him a hundred dollars and goes home with twenty five fish heads.

Two weeks later, he's back and this time he's really angry. "Marv," he says, "You are a crook! You're selling me these disgusting fish heads for $4 each and I just found out I can buy the whole fish for $2. You're ripping me off!"

With a big smile, Marv says, "See? You're smarter already!"

A fast thinking married guy

A masked bank robber bursts into a bank and forces the tellers at gunpoint to load a sack with all the cash they had in their tills. On his way out the door, a brave customer grabbed the robber's mask and pulled it off – revealing the robber's face. With no hesitation whatsoever, the robber shot and killed the customer.

The robber looked around the bank and after noticing one of the tellers looking straight at him, shot her as well. Everyone else, by now, very afraid looked down at the floor in silence.

The robber yelled out, "Anybody else in here see my face?"

After a few moments of intense silence, one older man tentatively raised his hand and said, "My wife here got a pretty good look at you."

A fast thinking guy with a dog

Two guys are walking their dogs, a black Labrador Retriever and a Chihuahua. Passing a bar, the "Lab" walker says, "Let's go in and get a beer."

The Chihuahua guys says, "Don't be ridiculous. We can't take our dogs in there."

The Lab guy says, "Oh yeah. Watch this."

In he goes and orders a beer.

The bartender says, "Sorry, you can't bring your dog in here."

The Lab guy says, "But he's my Seeing Eye dog."

The bartender says, "Oh. Sorry. Here's your beer."

The Chihuahua guy follows him in and orders a beer.

The bartender says, "Sorry, you can't bring your dog in here."

The Chihuahua guy says, "But he's my Seeing Eye dog."

The bartender says, "Yeah, right. A Chihuahua? Give me a break."

The Chihuahua guy says, "They gave me a Chihuahua?!"

A fast thinking mental patient

A truck driver doing his usual delivery to the Institute of Mental Health discovered a flat tire just as he was about to head home. He jacked up the truck and took the flat tire off.

When he was about to put the spare on, he accidentally dropped all the bolts into the drain. When he could not fish the bolts out, he started to panic.

At that exact moment, a mental patient happened to walk past and asked the driver what happened. The frustrated truck driver described his predicament.

The patient laughed at him and said, "You can't even fix such a simple problem? Here's what you need to do. Take one bolt each from each of the other three tires and use them to bolt on this tire. Then drive slowly to the nearest workshop and replace the missing ones. It's as easy as that!"

The driver was very impressed and asked, "You're a pretty smart guy. What are you doing here in a mental institute?"

The patient replied, "I'm here because I'm crazy… not because I'm stupid!"

Fast thinking linguistics student

A linguistics professor was lecturing his class. "In English," he explained, "a double negative forms a positive. In some languages, such as Russian, a double negative is still a negative. However, there is no language wherein a double positive can form a negative."

A voice from the back of the room piped up, "Yeah… right."

A fast thinking interpreter

The Mafia was looking for a new man to make weekly collections from all the private businesses that they were '*protecting*.' Feeling the heat from the police force, they had decided to use a deaf person for this job figuring that if he were to get caught, he wouldn't be able to communicate to the police what he was doing.

On his first week, the deaf collector picks up over forty thousand dollars but he gets greedy, decides to keep the money and stashes it in a safe place. The Mafia soon realizes that their collection is late, and "the boys" send some muscle to "pay a visit" to the deaf collector.

The hoods find the deaf collector and ask him where the money is. Since the deaf collector can't communicate with them, the Mafia goons have brought along a professional sign language interpreter.

The Mafia hood says to the interpreter, "Ask him where da frickin' money is."

Using sign language, the interpreter asks, "Where - is - the - money?"

The deaf man signs him back, "I - don't - know - what - you - are - talking - about."

The interpreter tells the hood, "He says he doesn't know what you're talking about."

The hood pulls out a loaded 357 Magnum, sticks it in the ear of the deaf collector and pulls the hammer back.

Then he says to the interpreter, "Now ask him one more time where da frickin' money is."

The interpreter signs, "Where - is - the - money?"

The deaf man signs back, "The - $40,000 - is - hidden - in - a - tree - stump - in - my - back - yard."

The interpreter says to the hood, "He says he still doesn't know what you're talking about, and that you haven't got the guts to pull that trigger."

Fast thinking college professor

Two college students were sweating their chemistry final and as so often happens, on the night before the final, they decided to party instead of cramming for the big exam. As a result, they skipped the final but showed up after the exam telling the prof that their car had a flat tire and they were unable to get home in time to bone up for the final. Thus they would need more time to study.

The prof agreed and gave them an extra day and this time the boys crammed all night and walked into their final pretty well prepared.

The prof assigned them to separate rooms for their exam. Each kid shrugged and went off to the assigned room.

The 1st question for 5 points was to explain the concept of molarity. Easy.

The 2nd question worth 95 points was: Which tire was the flat one?

A fast thinking philosophy student

An eccentric philosophy professor gave a one question final exam after a semester that covered a broad range of philosophical thought. Once the class was seated and ready to go, the professor picked up his chair, plopped it on his desk and wrote on the board: "Using all the philosophical principles and thought that we have covered this semester, prove that this chair does not exist."

Fingers flew, erasers erased and notebooks were filled in furious fashion. Some students wrote over thirty pages in one hour attempting to refute the existence of the chair.

One member of the class however, handed in his completed answer less than a minute after the exam started.

Weeks later, when the grades were posted, the rest of the group marveled at the fact that he had been awarded an "A" when he had barely written anything at all.

All he wrote on his exam was: "What chair?"

A fast thinking economics student

Not expecting to do well on the economics exam, an economics student was heartened by the first question: In any given year, and to the nearest ton, how much wheat did the United States export?

Smiling confidently, he wrote: Year: 1492

Amount of wheat exported: None.

A fast-thinking cop

A policeman was being cross-examined by a defense attorney during a felony trial. The lawyer was trying to undermine the police officer's credibility:

Q: "Officer… did you see my client fleeing the scene?"

A: "No sir. But I subsequently observed a person matching the description of the offender, running several blocks away."

Q: "Officer, please tell the court who provided this description?"

A: "The officer who responded to the scene."

Q: "A fellow officer provided the description of this so-called offender eh? And do you trust your fellow officers?"

A: "Yes, sir. With my life."

Q: "With your life? Let me ask you this then officer. Do you have a room where you change clothes to get ready for your daily duties?"

A: "Yes sir, we do!"

Q: "And do you have a locker in that room?"

A: "Yes, sir. I do."

Q: "And do you have a lock on your locker?"

A: "Yes, sir."

Q: "Well then, officer, seeing as you trust your fellow officers with your life and all, why do you find it necessary to lock your locker in a room you share with these same officers?"

A: "Well sir… we share the building with the court complex, and sometimes lawyers have been known to walk through that room."

A fast-thinking guy from Oklahoma

An old Oklahoma rancher retired to Georgia where he had inherited a large farm. It was fixed up nice; picnic tables, horseshoe courts, basketball court, and it had a large pond in the back that was properly shaped and fixed up for swimming.

One evening he went down to the pond to check it over and as he neared the pond, he heard female type voices shouting and laughing. As he got there he saw a bunch of nubile, young women skinny dipping in his pond.

He coughed loudly to make the women aware of his presence and they all shrieked and went to the deep end of the pond. One of the women shouted, "We're not coming out until you leave!"

The old cowboy replied, "Now girls, don't you all fret none. I didn't come down here to watch you ladies swim naked or even make you get out of the pond naked. I'm just here to feed the alligator."

A fast thinking senior

A senior was going to bed one night when his wife told him that he had left the light on in the shed. As he looked for himself, he saw that there were people in the shed taking things. He phoned the police, and they told him that no one was in the area to help at this time, but they would send help as soon as they it was available.

He said "OK," hung up, and waited one minute, then phoned the police back; "Hello. I just called you a minute ago because there were people in my shed. Well, you don't have to worry about them now because I've just shot them."

Within five minutes there were half a dozen police cars in the area, an Armed Response unit; the works. Of course, they caught the burglars red-handed.

One of the officers said, "I thought you said that you shot them!"

The smiling, fast-thinking senior replied, "And I thought you said there was nobody available!"

A really slow thinker

An angel appears at a university faculty meeting and tells the dean that as a reward for his unselfish and exemplary behavior, the Lord has decided to reward him with his choice of infinite wealth, infinite wisdom, or infinite beauty.

Without hesitating, the dean selects infinite wisdom.

"Done!" says the angel, and disappears in a flash of light.

Now, all heads turn toward the dean, who sits omnisciently at the head of the boardroom table looking miserable. At length, one of his colleagues whispers, "Please share something wise with us, oh newly enlightened one."

The newly enlightened dean looks slowly around the room, sighs and then, with tears in his eyes, tells them, "I should have taken the money!"

A fast thinker or a slow thinker

An executive was interviewing a young woman for a position in his company. In order to find out something about her personality he asked her, "If you could have dinner with anyone–living or dead–who would it be?"

She replied, "The living one."

The fast thinking Hall of Fame

A young bachelor gets a date with a hot-looking travel agency manager who lives in a posh 40th story Manhattan penthouse. He is quite nervous when he goes to pick her up as he wants to make a great first impression. When she opened the door to invite him in, her little French Poodle, 'Fergie,' greeted him as well.

She told him, "I'm really sorry but I'm going to need just a few more minutes to finish getting ready. Would you mind playing with little Fergie here for a few minutes while I do that?"

"I'd be happy to," he gallantly offered.

She handed him a small rubber ball and said, "If he bothers you he loves to play fetch. Toss the ball for him and he'll go get it for you."

"No problem," the guy replied.

As soon as she left him alone, "cute" little Fergie started humping his leg so, he picked up the ball and tossed it gently across the living room. Fergie ran over, picked it up, returned it and then it was right back to the leg-humping.

A little bothered by this, he tossed the ball a little further. Same result. By now, the guy was more than a little irritated. Each time he would toss the ball a little further and each time the dog would bring it back and start humping his leg again.

Finally, in an act of frustration, he tossed the ball across the living room. It bounced once on the floor and then right through the open doorway, out on to the balcony and then, right over the balcony railing – only to be followed by Fergie, who proceeded to fall forty floors to a horrible death on the pavement below.

The guy ran out on the balcony and was stunned as he saw poor old Fergie's bloody carcass splattered all over the sidewalk below. He began to panic as he wondered how he would ever be able to explain the mishap to his date and still stand any chance at all of having a successful relationship with her.

A few minutes later, she came into the living room, smiling radiantly as she said, "Thank you so much for your patience. I hope that Fergie didn't cause you any trouble. Isn't he just the cutest, happiest little dog you ever saw?"

With a very solemn expression on his innocent-looking face, he told her, "Well, to tell you the truth, he seemed a little depressed to me."

Fast thinking thieves

Fred and Ethyl came out of the shopping mall with their packages and were shocked to find their car gone. Assuming it had been stolen they notified the police via cell phone and went inside to wait for the police to arrive.

Half an hour later a young detective drove them back to where their car had been parked to see if any evidence could be found at the scene of the crime. But, when they get there, their missing car is back in the exact spot with a note on the windshield along with two tickets to a concert attached. The note thanks them for the use of their car, and explained that the car-thief's wife was about to give birth and had to be rushed to the hospital - it even noted that his wife had a little boy.

Fred and Ethyl's faith in humanity is restored and they go to the concert and have a wonderful time.

They arrive home late that night to find their entire house robbed, with a note on the door reading: "Good one eh?

PS: Hope you enjoyed the concert."

A fast-thinking teacher

After retiring from the Canadian Armed Services, a former Gunnery Sergeant took a new job as a high school teacher in

Cudworth, Saskatchewan.

Just before the school year started, he injured his back and as a result he was required to wear a light plaster cast around the upper part of his body. Fortunately, the cast fit under his shirt and wasn't noticeable when he wore his suit coat.

On the first day of class, he found himself assigned to the toughest students in the school. The smart-ass punks, having already heard the new teacher was a former soldier, were leery of him and the teacher knew they would be testing his discipline in the classroom.

Walking confidently into the rowdy classroom, the new teacher opened the window wide and sat down at his desk. A strong breeze was blowing and it made his tie flap.

So… he picked up a stapler and stapled his tie to his chest.

The rest of the year went smoothly...

Winston Churchill

Lady Astor, England's first female politician, once said to Churchill, "Winston, you are a terrible man and if you were my husband, I'd poison your tea."

Churchill replied, "If you were my wife I'd drink it."

John Wilkes

John Wilkes, an English Politician, was told by a political opponent: "You sir, are an evil man and will most surely die by either the hangman's noose or some vile disease."

Wilkes replied, "That sir depends on whether I embrace your principals, or your mistress."

Edna Ferber

Author Michael Arlen on seeing Edna Ferber (author of Showboat)) in a double-breasted jacket: "Why, Edna, you look almost like a man."

To which Edna Ferber replied, "Why, Michael, so do you."

Ilka Chase

When told by a spiteful actress: "I enjoyed reading your book. Who wrote it for you?"

Author Ilka Chase replied: "Darling, I'm so glad that you liked it. Who read it to you?"

Chapter 4

Men vs. Women

When boys start to like girls

Mitchell and his pal Connor are sitting on the front porch talking when little Ella girl walks by. She turns and sticks her tongue out at them and says, "Boys are stupid!" Then she turns and walks away.

With a dreamy smile, Connor turns to Mitchell and says, "You know when it comes time for us to stop hating girls, she's the one I'm going to stop hating first."

Your basic anonymous married guy thoughts

* They say that over 50% of all marriages end in divorce – which isn't really so bad when you consider how the rest end.

* Being married is like sitting in a hot bathtub. After a while, it's not so hot.

* I have bad luck with relationships, every time I meet a girl I like, either she's married or I am.

* Getting married is very much like going to a restaurant with a bunch of your friends. You order what you want and then when you see what your buddy has, you wish you'd ordered that.

Why your basic guy likes to remain anonymous

* Standing at the bar during the wedding reception a man said to the man beside him, "You know what I did before I got married?"

The guy replied, "I have no idea."

With a sad face the man replied, "Anything I wanted to."

* Did you hear what happened to the guy after he asked his beautiful girlfriend to marry him and she said, "No?"

A: He lived happily ever after.

Mae West said

* "Too much of a good thing is wonderful."

* "Between two evils, I pick the one I've never tried before."

Charlotte Whitton said

"Whatever women must do they must do twice as well as men to be thought half as good. Luckily, this is not difficult."

H.L. Mencken said

"A man may be a fool and not know it, but... not if he is married."

Margaret Thatcher said

"In politics, if you want anything said, ask a man. If you want anything done, ask a woman."

Erica Jong said

"You see a lot of smart guys with dumb women, but you hardly ever see a smart woman with a dumb guy."

Mickey Rooney said

"Always get married in the morning. That way, if it doesn't work out, you haven't wasted a whole day."

Jack Benny said

"My wife Mary and I have been married for forty-seven years and not once have we had an argument serious enough to consider divorce: murder... yes. But divorce... never."

A great comeback

A couple drove down a country road for several miles, not saying a word. An earlier discussion had led to an argument and neither of them wanted to concede their position.

As they passed a barnyard of mules, goats and pigs, the husband asked sarcastically, "Relatives of yours?"

"As a matter of they are," the wife replied. She turned to him, smiled and continued, "They're my in-laws."

Your wife will love this

A man arrived home from work to find his wife standing at the door beside his packed bags and yelling at him, "Get out!!!"

As he walked away with his bags, she screamed, "I wish you a slow and painful death, you son of a bitch!"

With an exasperated look, he turned to her and said, "Okay... so now you want me to stay?"

What mothers of the bride love to do

Three days before the wedding, the bride-to-be calls her mother with some bad news. "Mom," she says, "I just found out that my fiancé's mother has bought the exact same dress as you to wear to the wedding."

The bride's mother thinks for a moment and says, "Don't worry dear. I'll just go and buy another dress to wear to the ceremony."

"But mother," says the bride, "that dress cost a fortune! What will you do with it? It's such a waste to not use it."

"Who said I won't use it?" her mother asked. "I'll just wear it to the rehearsal dinner."

The missing husband

A frantic woman approaches a policeman and says, "Officer, officer, oh please… you've got to help me. Please help me!"

The policeman says, "I'd be glad to ma'am, what's the problem?"

She says, "It's my poor, dear husband. He's missing!"

The policeman says, "Okay ma'am, I understand. Now, just calm down and tell me when and where you last saw him."

"Well," she says, "He went out to get a newspaper three days ago and I haven't seen him since. Oh please, please… you've just got to help me find him."

The policeman assured her, "I'd be glad to help you find him ma'am. Could you please describe him for me?"

"Well," she said, "he's bald. He's short and he's fat. He's kind of ugly and he sweats a lot, plus he spits when he's talking."

As she said that, she paused for a moment, slowly shook her head and then added, "On second thought… never mind."

The fortune teller

In a dark and hazy room, peering into a crystal ball, the fortune teller delivered grave news, "There's no easy way to tell you this, so I'll just be blunt. Prepare yourself to be a widow. Your husband is going to die a violent and horrible death this year."

Visibly shaken, Ethyl stared at the mystic's ancient face, then at the single flickering candle, then down at her hands. She took a few deep breaths to compose herself and also to stop her mind racing. She simply had to know.

She met the fortune teller's gaze, steadied her voice and asked, "Will I be acquitted?"

Agatha Christie

"An archeologist is the best husband a woman can have. The older she gets, the more interested he is in her."

Why women are stupid

A frustrated man said to his wife, "I don't know how you can be so stupid and yet so beautiful at the same time."

She responded with, "Okay sweetheart. Now listen very carefully and I'll explain it to you. It's really quite simple. You see, God made me beautiful so that you would be attracted to me but then… God went ahead and made me stupid so that I would be attracted to you!"

Why men are stupid

A guy is having a beer with his buddy and complains to him, "I came home from the golf course today to find that the wife had left a note on the fridge. It said, 'It's not working! I can't take it anymore! Gone to stay with my Mother.'

I opened the fridge, the light came on, and the beer was cold… what the hell is she talking about?"

A married woman's ways

A woman was complaining to the neighbor about her husband's nasty habit of coming home late. No matter what she did, she could not change him.

Her neighbor advised her, "You should try doing what I did. Two years ago, I heard my husband coming home at three o'clock in the morning. From my bed, I called out: 'Is that you, Stan?' That sure cured him."

The woman was a little skeptical and said, "It did?"

"I'll say it did," she replied with a sinister smile, "His name is Phil."

Helen Rowland said

"Before marriage, a man will lie awake all night thinking about something you said.

After marriage, he'll fall asleep before you finish saying it."

How men lose arguments

A man and his wife are having an argument and the man becomes so frustrated he tells her, "I was a fool when I married you!"

She tells him, "I know but I was in love and I didn't notice it."

A few seconds later she added, "But my mother did."

Buddy Hacket said

"Beauty may only be skin deep but ugly… is to the bone."

How *some* women handle the anger thing

A husband and wife are sharing a bottle of wine on their anniversary and he asks her, "One of the things that amazes me about you is that you never argue with me when I get mad at you. How do you always control yourself so well?"

She replied, "That's easy sweetheart. Whenever you get mad and yell at me, I just go and clean the toilet?"

Puzzled, he asks, "How does that help?"

Smiling sweetly, she replies, "I use your toothbrush."

The High School Reunion

A reluctant husband agrees to accompany his wife back to her hometown to attend her high school reunion. After going through the ritual of meeting several of her friends and former school mates, they are sitting at a table where by now he is yawning and overly bored. The band starts up and people are beginning to dance.

There's a guy on the dance floor living it up large: break dancing, moon walking, back flips, buying drinks for people, the works.

The woman turns to her husband and says, "See that guy over there doing all the wild dancing?"

With a bored look he tells her, "Yeah."

She tells him, "Well, twenty five years ago he proposed to me and I turned him down."

With an evil smile he says, "It looks like he's still celebrating!!!"

Why it's not fun to golf with the wife

A husband and wife are on the 9th green when suddenly she collapses from a heart attack. "Help me dear," she groans.

The husband calls 911 on his cell phone, talks for a few minutes then picks up his putter, and starts to line up his putt. His wife raises her head off the green and yells at him, "I'm dying here and you're putting?"

"Don't worry dear," says the husband calmly, "they found a doctor on the second hole and he's coming to help you.

"Well, how long will it take for him to get here?" she asks feebly.

"It shouldn't be too long at all," says her husband. "Everybody's going to let him play through."

Priorities

A man who managed to get a seat right behind third base at Game 7 of the World Series was surprised to find that the seat beside him was empty. A sweet little old lady sat on the other side of the empty seat and at the end of the second inning the man told her he was surprised to find such a great seat empty for such an important game.

The little old lady replied, "Oh that seat belongs to my husband. We've had these two seats for almost forty years now."

"Well why didn't he come to the game?" the man asked.

"He's dead," was the reply.

"Oh... I am so sorry to hear that. But why didn't you give his seat to one of his good friends or another family member?"

With a disarmingly sweet smile, she replied, "They're all at the funeral."

Eleanor Roosevelt

"You wouldn't worry so much about what other people think of you if you realized how seldom they do."

Tallulah Bankhead

"If I had to live my life again I'd make all the same mistakes... only sooner."

The first fight

Three weeks after her wedding day, Sarah called her mother in a total panic. "Mom," she wailed, "John and I just had an absolutely horrible fight!"

"Calm down, Sarah," said her mother. "It's not half as bad as you think it is. Every marriage has to have its first fight!"

"I know that mother," said Sarah, "but what I don't know is... what I'm supposed to do with the body?"

That first awkward moment for newlyweds

Muldoon gets married and takes his bride to Las Vegas for their honeymoon. As they are checking in to Caesar's Palace, a tall, gorgeous brunette came strolling up to the counter, put her arms around Muldoon and said, "Well if it isn't my darling Muldoon, how nice to see you sweetheart."

Then she gave him a very passionate kiss. After the kiss she walked away looking over her shoulder as she said, "See you later big fella."

Later in their hotel room, Muldoon's furious bride asks him, "What the hell was that all about in the lobby?"

Muldoon says, "Hey, don't start in on me with that okay. I'm going to have a tough enough time as it is explaining you… to her!"

Ann Richards

"Ginger Rogers did everything Fred Astaire did. She just did it backwards while wearing high heels."

A license to kill

A nice, calm and respectable lady walked into a pharmacy, went right up to the pharmacist, looked straight into his eyes, and said, "I would like to buy some cyanide."

The pharmacist asked, "Why in the world would you need to buy any cyanide?"

The lady replied, "I need it to poison my husband."

The shocked pharmacist pulled back in horror and exclaimed, "I can't sell you any cyanide to kill your husband! That's against the law! I'll lose my license and they'll throw us both in jail! Absolutely not!"

The lady reached into her purse and pulled out a picture of her husband in a passionate embrace with the pharmacist's wife.

The pharmacist looked at the picture and replied, "Well that's different. You didn't tell me you had a prescription!"

Archie Bunker on what keeps a marriage together

"The only thing that holds a marriage together is the husband being big enough to step back and see where the wife is wrong."

Burning the dinner

A woman says to her husband when he comes home from work, "Darling, I have good news and bad news for you. First of all… I burned the dinner."

He says, "That's okay. Now then what's the bad news?"

Johnny Carson's favourite divorce joke

A very old couple went to visit a lawyer who asked them, "What can I do for you today?"

"We want to get a divorce," said the man.

The lawyer was incredulous, "A divorce! You can't be serious! How old are you?"

"I'm ninety three, she's ninety two and we've been married for seventy five years," he replied.

With a scowl, she glares daggers at him and adds, "Hated each other's guts for every minute of that time too."

"Well if that's the case, why have you waited until now to get a divorce?" the lawyer asked.

The old man replied, "We thought it would be best if we waited until the kids were dead."

Male sensitivity

Freddy's wife was dying, and poor Freddie was right there beside her deathbed - sobbing and overcome with grief.

As he cried, his wife patted his hand and said to him, "Freddie my darling, I know this all seems like such a terrible loss to you now, but please keep in mind that time is a great healer and soon, I am sure, you will find another wife."

Freddy sobs as he replies, "I know that sweetheart! But what am I going to do tonight?"

Good or bad news depends on your perspective

A man comes home from work and says to his wife, "Darling, I have some good news and some bad news for you.

First of all, I'm leaving you and running away with your best friend Ethyl."

She says, "That's wonderful. Now what's the bad news?"

A failure to communicate

A wife asks her husband, "Could you please go shopping for me and buy one carton of milk, and if they have eggs... get six."

A short time later the husband comes back with six cartons of milk. The wife asks him, "Why did you buy six cartons of milk?"

He replied, "Duh... hello sweetheart... they had eggs."

How to stay a bachelor

Sitting at the end of the bar, a guy tells the bartender that he is drinking in order to wash away the heartache of his broken engagement.

"That's too bad. What happened?" the bartender asked.

"Let me ask you a question. Would you marry someone who didn't know the meaning of the word faithful… someone who was flippant and even turned vicious when the subject of fidelity came up?"

"No way!" replied the bartender.

With a smile of relief the guy says, "Well, neither would she."

What a guy does with his old clothes

A woman is having lunch with a friend who is trying to convince her to give some used clothing to the Goodwill organization.

When she declined, her friend asked, "What does your husband do with all his old clothes?"

The wife replied, "He wears them!"

Yuppie values

Two yuppie ladies are having lunch and they started to talk about their husbands.

Muffy says, "That Biff is so terrible, it seems all we do is fight anymore. I've lost fifteen pounds."

Elspeth asks her, "Well why don't you just leave him?"

Muffy tells her, "I'm going to but I'd like to lose another fifteen pounds first."

Newlywed confusion

A new wife is eagerly preparing her first dinner for her new husband. As he starts to eat it, she tells him, "Sweetheart, I only know how to cook two things; beef stew and cherry pie."

He tells her, "That's wonderful honey. Which one is this?"

How to make the other guy happy

A couple is lying in bed. The woman says, "Sweetheart, I am going to make you the happiest man in the world."

The man says, "That is wonderful news darling. And I want you to know… I'm really going to miss you."

Getting off to the right start

A beautiful bride is walking down the aisle. Her groom is waiting for her, smiling and looking good in his tuxedo. She notices his golf bag with all his clubs beside him and asks, "Sweetheart, why did you bring your golf clubs?"

He replies, "This isn't going to take all day is it?"

Happy anniversary dear

A man, celebrating his 50th wedding anniversary was sitting at the head table with his wife on one side and his best friend, who was also his lawyer, on the other side. As the evening wore on, the lawyer noticed that the guest of honor was crying.

He asks him, "Fred, what's the matter old friend? This is an occasion that should bring a man great joy… not sadness."

Fred tearfully replied, "Do you remember twenty five years ago at our 25th anniversary when I told you that I hated her guts and that I was going to kill her?"

"I most certainly do! I talked you out of it."

"That's right, you talked me out of it you door knob by telling me that if I did it, I'd go to prison for twenty five years."

"Right! I talked you out of doing something that would have put you in the slammer for twenty five years. I did a good thing for you. So then tell me… why are you so unhappy?"

With another tearful outburst Fred replied, "Because today I'd be getting out of jail!"

5 major differences between men & women

1: A man will pay $2 for a $1 item he needs.

   A woman will often pay $1 for a $2 item that she doesn't need.

2: A woman will worry about the future until she gets a husband

   A man never worries about the future until he gets a wife.

3: A married man easily forgets his mistakes.

   A married woman never forgets his mistakes.

4: A successful man makes more money than his wife can spend.

   A successful woman finds a man who can do this.

5: A woman marries a man thinking she can change him.

   A man marries a woman hoping she'll never change.

Why do married men die before their wives?

A: They want to

Be careful what you wish for

A man was sitting alone in his office one night when a genie popped up out of his ashtray, "…and what will your third wish be?"

The man told the genie, "What? How can I be getting a third wish if I haven't even had a first or a second wish?"

"You have had two wishes already," the genie assured, "but your second wish was for me to put everything back the way it was before you made your first wish. Thus, you remember nothing because everything is the way it was before you made your first wish. You now have but one wish left."

"Okay," said the man, "I don't believe this, but what the heck. I've always wanted to understand women. I'd love to know exactly what's going on inside their heads."

"That's funny," said the genie as it granted his wish and disappeared forever, "That was your first wish, too!"

Understanding the female persona

A guy walking along the beach near San Francisco picks up an old bottle he finds in the sand. When he rubs it to remove the sand, a genie appears and tells him, "Thank you for releasing me from that horrible bottle. As a token of my gratitude, I will grant you one wish. Anything you want."

The man thinks for a moment and then says, "I've always wanted to go to Hawaii, but I'm afraid to fly. So my wish is, to go to Hawaii, first class and all expenses paid of course, but I don't want to fly."

The genie replies, "Okay, I can get you there on a boat."

The guy says, "No… that won't work. I get seasick. You'll have to come up with another way to get me there."

The genie says, "Well, if you don't go by air or by boat and we can't go by train so how do you expect me to get you there?"

The guy replies, "Well… you could build me a bridge and have me driven there in one of those luxury motorhomes."

The genie says, "A bridge! Are you nuts? It's well over two thousand miles from San Francisco to Hawaii. It's the Pacific Ocean! It's way too deep! There is absolutely no way it could be done. Please, ask me for anything else but that."

The guy thinks for a moment and then says, "Okay. I'm just recently divorced and I've never ever been able to even come close to understanding what women are really all about. And by that I mean, they are a total mystery to me.

Could you please explain to me what the heck women are all about? I want to understand what's really going on with them?"

The genie thinks for a moment and then says, "Okay then. Now, would you like a two lane bridge or a four lane bridge?"

The genie and the divorced guy

This guy is walking on the beach and he sees an old bottle. He picks it up and rubs it to clean off the sand and - poof! - a genie appears.

The genie says, "Thank you for releasing me from my prison. In my gratitude, I will grant you three wishes."

The genie pauses and then says, "But… wait a moment. I sense that you were married and are now divorced. Is this true?"

"Yes. That is true," the man replied.

"Well then according to the rules, whatever I give you, I will have to give double to your ex-wife."

The guy thought for a moment and then said, "OK. For my first wish, I would like ten million dollars."

"So it shall be done," said the genie. "But keep in mind… your ex-wife will get twenty million dollars."

"That's fine. For my second wish, I want a luxurious villa in Tahiti."

"So it shall be done," said the genie, "But your ex-wife will get two villas; one in Greece and one in Switzerland."

"That's okay," the guy says and his face lights up in a huge grin as he says, "For my third wish, I want you to beat me... half to death!"

Mother of the groom

A young man happily tells his mother he's finally fallen in love and is going to get married.

She is very excited by this and tells him, "That's wonderful dear. When can I meet her?"

He tells her, "Just for the fun of it, I'm coming over for lunch tomorrow and I'm bringing three women with me. I want you to guess which one I'm going to marry."

The mother agrees.

The next day, he brings three pretty good looking women over to his mom's place for lunch. They chat for a while and then she serves them all a nice lunch. During lunch when his mother heads to the kitchen to get coffee, he excuses himself and follows her into the kitchen where he asks her, "Okay, mom, which of those lovely ladies do you think I'm going to marry."

She immediately replies, "The redhead in the middle."

"Mother, you are truly amazing. You're right. How did you know?"

With a spiteful smile she replied, "I don't like her."

Just like the gal that married dear old Dad

Drew and Guy, are having a few drinks and Drew asked Guy how his love-life was going.

Drew replied, "My love-life is terrible. I don't think I'm ever going to find the right girl and get married. Every time I meet a girl I really like, I take her home to meet my parents and my mom just hates her."

Guy says, "Well, that's easy to solve. Just find a girl that's a lot like your mom and when you take her home to meet your parents, your mom will be able to identify with her and that way she'll grow to love her... problem solved!"

Drew mulls over the idea then says, "You know, that's a pretty good idea. It just might work. I think I'll try it. Thanks."

Six months later Guy asks Drew, "So, how's your love life?"

Drew says, "Oh, the same as always. I did try your idea out though. I met this great girl. She was a lot like my mom; same height and hair colour... even the same colour of eyes. She had the same physical mannerisms, even the same expressions as my mom, and my mom just loved her."

Guy says, "So then... why didn't you marry her?"

Drew says, "My dad hated her."

How long does it really last?

A woman says to her husband as he sits on the couch watching Sportsline, "You once told me you were going to spend your whole life trying to make me happy. What happened to that?"

He tells her, "I didn't expect to live this long."

Blondes and wallpaper

Marylou decided to redecorate her bedroom and wasn't sure how many rolls of wallpaper she would need. She knew that her friend Sylvia, who lived next door, had recently done the same job and the two rooms were identical in size. So, she called Sylvia and asked her, "How many rolls of wallpaper did you buy to do your bedroom?"

"Ten," said Sylvia.

Armed with that information, Marylou went out and bought ten rolls of paper. But after the job was done, she had two rolls left over.

She called Sylvia and told her, "Sylvia! I bought ten rolls of wallpaper for my bedroom, but I've got two leftover!"

"Really?" said Sylvia. "So did I."

A good joke to tell your wife

A funeral service is being held in a synagogue for a woman who has just passed away. After the service, as the pallbearers are carrying the casket out to the hearse, they accidentally bump into a wall, jarring the casket and from inside the casket they hear a faint moan.

They open it and find that the woman is actually alive. She lives for ten more years and then dies... again!

A ceremony is again held at the same synagogue. At the end of the ceremony, the same pallbearers are once again enlisted to carry the casket out to the hearse.

As they pick up the casket and begin the procession, the husband cries out, "Watch out for the wall!"

My mother's favourite joke

At a cocktail party, Phil is introduced by the host to a lovely woman, "Phil, I'd like you to meet Virginia Keelan."

As she offers her hand, Phil is struck by a magnificent diamond ring. He takes her hand and tells her, "Very pleased to meet you Virginia and may I tell you... that is a very beautiful diamond ring you are wearing."

Virginia tells him, "Why thank you Phil. It is a magnificent ring. It has been in my husband's family for six generations. It is known far and wide as the Keelan Diamond and in fact it actually has an old curse attached to it."

"Really. How very interesting. Would you mind if I asked you what this curse might be?"

Virginia smiles ruefully, "That would be Mr. Keelan."

Marital advice from a Rabbi

A man tells his Rabbi, "Rabbi, something terrible is happening to me and I need I should talk to you about it."

The Rabbi asked, "What's wrong?"

He replied, "It's my wife. She's poisoning me."

The Rabbi, very surprised by this, asks, "Are you sure about this?"

The man says, "I'm telling you, I'm certain. What should I do?"

The Rabbi then offers, "I'll tell you what. You should let me talk to her, I'll see what I can find out and then I'll let you know."

A week later the Rabbi calls the man and says, "Well, I called your wife yesterday. She talked to me on the phone for three hours. My advice to you is this… you should take the poison."

A case for always telling your wife the truth

A man phones home from the office and asks his wife, "Sweetheart, I have just been given the chance to go fishing for a week in Montana at a corporate retreat and schmooze with some of the top brass. It's a great opportunity for me to move up the corporate ladder. Would you please pack my clothes, my fishing equipment, and especially my blue silk pajamas? I'll be home in an hour to pick them up."

Half an hour later he stops by the house, grabs everything and rushes off.

A week later, he returns and his wife asks him, "So how was the trip darling? Did you have fun?"

He tells her, "Oh yes… it was great! But sweetheart, you forgot to pack my blue silk pajamas."

"No I didn't," she said. "I put them in your tackle box!"

Don't ask… don't tell

A man asks his wife, "Honey… if I died, do you think you'd get married again?"

She tells him, "Probably. I don't want to spend the rest of my life all alone."

He tells her, "Fair enough. But would you and your new husband continue to live in this house?"

She says, "Probably. I mean it's paid for and everything."

He says, "Okay, I can understand that. But would you let him sleep in our bed?"

She says, "Well that's kind of a ridiculous question don't you think? I mean, after all… it's just a bed."

He says, "Right. I can see your point. So then… would you let him use my golf clubs?"

She says, "No. Definitely not… he's left-handed."

Marital priorities

A guy finally married his long-time girlfriend. One evening, after the honeymoon, he was cleaning his golf shoes. His wife was standing there watching him and after a long period of silence she finally said, "Honey, I've been thinking, now that we are married I think it's time you quit golfing. Maybe you should sell your golf clubs."

He gets this horrified look on his face.

She says, "Darling, what's wrong?"

"There for a minute you were sounding like my ex-wife."

"Ex-wife!" she screams, "You never told me you were married before!"

He screams right back, "I wasn't!"

Brains or beauty

This guy is sitting at home alone when he hears a knock on the front door. He opens it to find two sheriff's deputies standing there. One of the deputies asks if he is married, and if so, does he have a picture of his wife.

The guy says, "Sure, wait here just a minute," and goes to get a picture of his wife which he hands to one of the deputies.

The deputies take the picture back to their car and scan it in to their computer. They return a few minutes later to hand the photo back to the guy, telling him, "I'm sorry to have to tell you this sir, but it looks like your wife's been hit by a truck."

The guy says, "I know that, but she has a great personality and she's an excellent cook."

Rita Rudner

* Before I met my husband I'd never fallen in love, though I'd stepped in it a few times.

* My boyfriend and I broke up. He wanted to get married and I didn't want him to.

* When I meet a man, I ask myself, "Is this the man I want my children to spend their weekends with?"

* I love being married. It is so great to find that special person you want to annoy for the rest of your life.

* My husband and I are either going to buy a dog or have a child. We can't decide whether to ruin our carpet or our lives.

* Neurotics build castles in the air, psychotics live in them. My mother cleans them.

* In Hollywood a marriage is a success if it outlasts milk.

The wit (and Wisdom) of Phyllis Diller

* Housework can't kill you, but I figure, why take a chance?

* Never go to bed mad. Stay up and fight.

* I want my children to have all the things I couldn't afford. Then I want to move in with them.

A bum rap for the ladies

Former Houston Oilers coach Bum Phillips was asked by Bob Costas why he takes his wife on all the road trips.

Phillips responded: "Because she's too ugly to kiss good-bye."

A love story

It was Christmas Eve and the mall was packed. A man and his wife were doing some last-minute shopping. As the wife walked through the mall, she was surprised to look up and see that her husband was nowhere to be seen. She was quite distressed by this because they had a lot to do so she called him on her mobile phone to ask him where he was.

In a calm voice, the husband said, "Honey, you remember that jewelry store we went into about 5 years ago where you fell in love with that diamond necklace that we could not afford and I told you that I would get it for you one day?"

The wife choked up and tears came to her eyes as she remembered the incident clearly. She said, "Yes darling, I remember that jewelry store… very well."

He said, "Great… I'm in the bar right next to it."

The handsome prince and the frog

Once upon a time… there was a handsome prince who lived in a fabulous castle. One day, he was out for a walk by the river and he came upon a frog.

The frog said to the handsome prince, "Oh handsome prince, I was once a beautiful princess until an evil witch cast a spell on me and turned me into a frog.

However, one kiss from a handsome prince–like yourself–will turn me back into a beautiful princess. Then you and I can get married and move into your castle with my mother where you can look after us and share your wealth with me, be totally faithful to me forever and be deliriously happy doing so."

As the prince picked up the frog and then reared back and fired it as far out into the river as he could, he muttered, "I don't think so."

A dog or a wife?

1: The later you are, the more excited a dog is to see you.

2: Dogs don't notice if you call them by another dog's name.

3: Dogs like it if you leave a lot of things on the floor.

4: A dog's parents never visit.

5: Dogs agree that you have to raise your voice to get your point across.

6: Dogs find you amusing when you're drunk.

7: Dogs like to go hunting and fishing.

8: A dog will never wake you up in the middle of the night to ask, "If I died, would you get another dog?"

9: If a dog has babies, you can put an ad in the paper and either sell them or give them away.

10: A dog will let you put a studded collar on it without calling you a pervert.

11: If a dog smells another dog on you they don't get mad, they just think it's interesting.

12: If a dog leaves you it won't take half your stuff and then take you to court and try to get the other half.

One more dog question

If your dog is barking at the back door and your wife is yelling at the front door, who do you let in first?

A: The dog, of course. He'll shut up once you let him in.

The perfect shot

Harry stood over his tee shot on the 450 yard 18th hole for what seemed an eternity. He waggled, looked up, looked down, waggled again, but still didn't start his back swing.

Finally Dick, his exasperated partner asked, "Harry, what the hell is taking you so long?"

"My wife is watching me from the clubhouse balcony," Harry

explained. "I want to make a perfect shot."

Dick said, "Now Harry, that's just about the dumbest thing I've ever heard you say. There's no way you can hit her from here."

A sad day or what?

Marvin - Clara's much older husband - has just been buried after drowning in their swimming pool. Two weeks later Clara meets her friend Ethyl for lunch at their country club.

Ethyl tells Clara, "Oh dear Clara, I'm so sorry to hear that poor Marvin died. I certainly hope he left you enough to get by?"

With a smile, Clara says, "Oh yes... he certainly did. My poor sweet Marvin left me over twenty million dollars."

Ethyl replies, "Oh my dear... that's wonderful... especially when you realize that Marvin couldn't read or even write."

With an evil smile, Clara says, "Yes... and unfortunately for poor old Marv, he wasn't much of a swimmer either."

Proof that guys can be stupid - really stupid

A guy was sitting quietly reading his paper when his wife walked up behind him and whacked him on the head with a frying pan.

"What the hell was that for?" he asked.

"That was for the piece of paper in your pants pocket with the name Mary Lou written on it," she replied.

With a sheepish grin he said, "You don't have to worry about that sweetheart. It's very simple. Last week I went to the races and Mary Lou was the name of one of the horses I bet on. That's all."

Well that worked. "Oh honey... I'm so sorry I hit you with that frying pan. I should have known there was a good explanation."

Three days later he was watching a ball game on TV when she walked up and hit him in the head again, this time with the iron skillet, which knocked him out cold.

When he came to, he asked, "What the heck was that for?"

She replied "Your horse called."

Henny Youngman's secret to a successful marriage

"A happy marriage like ours doesn't just happen. We both make a real effort and take the time to nurture our love so that we can grow together as a couple.

For example; we take one night a week and go to a nice little restaurant for a romantic, candlelight dinner. We have some fine wine, great food and lots of romantic talk.

Then there's music and dancing, followed by a long, passionate night making love. She goes Tuesdays and I go Thursdays."

Bill Hicks on women

"I've learned a lot about women. I think I've learned exactly how the fall of man occurred in the Garden of Eden.

Adam and Eve were in the Garden of Eden, and Adam said one day, 'Wow, Eve, here we are, at one with nature, at one with God, we'll never age, we'll never die, and all our dreams come true the instant that we have them.'

And Eve said, 'Yeah... it's just not enough is it?'"

Mrs. Hughes secret to a long marriage

"People ask me all the time, 'What's the secret to a long and happy marriage?'

Well, I'm not sure about the secret to a happy marriage but I can tell you what the secret to a long one is. The secret is children. The only reason my husband and I are together today is because of our kids... neither of us wanted custody!"

The crow's nest

This guy brings his golf buddy home, unannounced, for dinner.

His wife goes crazy and starts screaming at him while his friend sits there shocked listening to the tirade: "My hair and makeup are not done, the house is a friggin' mess and I'm still in my pajamas. I can't be bothered with cooking tonight! Why did you decide to bring one of your stupid friends home un-announced you stupid idiot?"

The husband calmly replies, "Because when we were out on the golf course today he told me he's thinking of getting married."

Every married man will ask

"If a man speaks in the forest and there is no one around who can hear him... is he still wrong?'

The famous lawyer Clarence Darrow once said...

The first half of our life is ruined by our parents.

The second half is ruined by our children.

Chapter 5

Drinking Stories

Dylan Thomas' definition of an alcoholic

Someone you don't like who drinks as much as you do.

The difference between a drunk and an alcoholic

A drunk doesn't have to go to meetings.

The nerve of some people's kids

A travelling salesman, who has run out of gas on a street in the suburbs, pulls his car over to the curb. As he gets out of the car, he hears very loud rock'n roll music coming from inside a house across the street and assuming that someone must be home; he goes up and knocks on the door.

An eleven-year old boy, wearing a black, silk smoking jacket complete with a white ascot, answers the door. He has a martini in one hand and a big cigar in the other.

The man looks inside and notices that there are five of the kid's buddies sitting around a table; drinking martinis, smoking cigars and playing poker. Half a dozen girls in various stages of undress are dancing and running around.

He asks the kid, "Are your parents home?"

The kid smiles and takes a leisurely sip of his martini followed by a long slow drag on the cigar.

Then he looks the salesman right in the eye and says, "What do you think?"

The nerve of some people's kids 2

A twelve year old walks into a bar and asks the waitress for a boilermaker. She says to him, "What are you? Nuts? You're just a kid. You wanna get me in trouble or something?"

He tells her, "Maybe later baby. But for right now just be a good girl and get me my drink!"

How do you know a dead man was a real drinker?

When he's cremated, his body burns for a week.

The original shaggy dog story

Ted goes into a bar with Fred, his cocker spaniel and orders a beer. When the bartender brings it over, Ted downs it and says, "I'll bet you a beer that my very smart, talking dog Fred here can answer any question you ask him."

Looking skeptically down his nose at Fred, the bartender says, "You're on," and pours him another beer.

Ted tosses it back and says, "Okay, ask him anything."

Pointing toward the ceiling, the bartender asks, "What's that up there?"

"Wroof," replies the dog.

The bartender is not impressed and tells Ted, "Aw cummon! That's a crock! Lemme ask him another question."

"Okay but it'll cost you another beer," replies Ted.

Glaring at him, the bartender says, "Alright… but this time, I'm going to ask a tougher question."

Looking Fred the dog right in the eye, the bartender asks, "Who was the greatest baseball player in history?"

Fred the dog looks at him and barks, "Wruth."

The infuriated bartender says, "Oh… a real smart guy eh? Well that's it for you and your stupid talking dog act!"

Then he picks Ted and his dog Fred up by the scruff of their necks and tosses them right out the door onto the street.

As Ted lays there in the gutter, Fred the dog walks over to him and asks, "Was it Joe DiMaggio?"

Knowing when to quit

Four guys are sitting at a bar drinking boilermakers when suddenly one guy leans back in his bar stool and falls right back on the floor where he lies… perfectly still… out like a light.

One of the other guys says, "Boy, y'a gotta hand it to ole Freddy boy there… he knows when to stop drinking."

A drunk goes to confession

A drunk staggers out of a bar and wanders into a large church. He finds a confessional, goes in and sits down. After sitting there for a few moments in silence, the priest who is hearing confessions asks,

"May I help you my son."

The drunk says, "You sure can. Have you got any toilet paper?"

The cockeyed pessimist

Two friends meet for a drink. One of them was looking rather forlorn and down in the mouth so his pal asked him, "What's with the sad face? You look like the whole world caved in?"

The sad guy replied, "Well... for starters, three weeks ago, an uncle died and left me ten thousand dollars."

"I'm sorry to hear about the death, but that's a bit of good luck for you, eh?"

"Hold on, I'm just getting started. Two weeks ago, a cousin I never knew was killed in a car accident and left me twenty thousand, free and clear."

"Well, that's a sad story but still... you did all right by it. You can't be too disappointed by that!"

"No. That part was okay. But then, last week my grandfather passed away. I inherited almost one hundred thousand dollars."

"Incredible... so then... how come you look so sad?"

"Well, so far this week... nothing!"

A drunk from Boston

A very drunk guy boards a bus in Boston one Sunday morning and makes his way to the first empty seat. He plops his disgusting self down beside a very matronly and very sober older woman who is on her way home from church. She gets one whiff of the guy, wrinkles her nose in disgust and says, "Young man. You are going straight to hell!"

With a look of utter dismay on his face, the drunk looks up and says, "Aw man! I'm on the wrong bus!"

The art of the question

A man sits down at the bar and orders a beer. Sitting beside him is a nice-looking lady and on the floor beside her is a dog. The guy asks the nice-looking lady, "Excuse me ma'am, but does your dog bite?"

She smiles and tells him, "No. He's very friendly."

Encouraged by this, he bends down to pet the dog and the dog bites him.

He jumps back and with a surprised look he says to the lady, "I thought you said your dog didn't bite!"

She smiles and tells him, "That's not my dog."

Irish priorities

Murphy was staggering home with a pint of booze in his back pocket when he slipped and fell heavily. Struggling to his feet, he felt something wet running down his leg. "Please Lord," he implored, "let it be blood!!"

The evils of drinking

It's midnight and a very drunk man is staggering along a side street when he is stopped by a policeman who asks him where he is going.

Slurring his words the drunk tells him, "Occifer, I just happen to be on my way to listen to a lecture about the terrible effects of alcohol abuse on the human body and society in general."

The skeptical policeman replies, "Really now? And just who is going to be giving a lecture like that at this time of night?"

The man replies, "My wife!"

Finding Jesus

A drunk on the tail end of a week-long bender stumbles across a baptismal service on Sunday afternoon down by the river. He staggers down into the water, trips and goes right under the water.

He comes up standing next to the preacher who turns to him and says, "Welcome brother... are you ready to find Jesus?"

The drunk says, "Yes Preacher... I am. I purely am."

The preacher then dunks the fellow under the water and pulls him right back up. "Have you found Jesus?" he asked.

"Nooo, I haven't!" said the drunk.

So... the preacher dunks him under again: this time for a little bit longer.

When he finally brings him back up he asks, "Now brother, tell us... have you found Jesus?"

The sputtering drunk replies, "Noooo, I have not Reverend."

The frustrated preacher dunks him again and this time he holds the man under for quite a bit longer... almost a full minute.

When he brings him out of the water he says in a very harsh tone,

"My God brother! Have you found Jesus yet?"

The poor old drunk is nearly drowned as he gasps for air, wipes his eyes and then finally says to the preacher, "I'm sorry preacher. I have not found him. Are you sure this is where he fell in?"

A drunk and a lobster

A drunk goes into his favourite tavern, puts a live, five-pound, Maine lobster on the bar and tells the bartender, "Joseph, my life-long buddy, for all these years of your most excellent service, I want you to have this fine Maine lobster as a token of my appreciation."

The bartender tells him, "Thanks a lot. I'll take it home for dinner."

"No, no. You don't have to do that!" the drunk said. "He's already had dinner, but I'll bet he'd love to go to the movies."

A unique pick-up technique

A man walks into a bar, orders himself a drink and then with drink in hand, strolls up to this fine-looking lady and starts talking to her. In due course, she asks him what he does for a living.

He puffs up his chest and in his most macho voice, tells her, "I used to be a lumberjack in the Sahara Desert!"

She laughs, "The Sahara Desert.... right! Don't be ridiculous! There aren't any trees in the Sahara Desert."

With an air of great confidence he replies, "Yeah... sure... now there aren't!"

White Irish Drinkers

An Irishman, well into his cups, is sitting at the bar in a Chicago pub. He turns to the man next to him and says, "Yer lovely accent suggests to me that ye might be from Ireland so tell me now... could that possibly be true?"

"And sure it is oy am," replied the man... half in the bag himself.

"Awww now... that's just delightful to hear.... just delightful. So tell me then, what part of the Emerald Isle would ye be from?"

"Why oy'm from the grandest city in all of the Emerald Isle... Dublin itself."

"Saints preserve us! Oy'm from Dublin meself! Tell me then laddie, what part of Dublin are ye from?"

"Oy was born and raised right on Killarney Street."

"Faith and begora, I don't believe it. Why laddie… oy meself was born and raised on that very same street!"

He put his arm around his new friend's shoulder and said, "Ye know, I've a grand feelin' oy should know ye…."

Just then a guy walks up to the bar and says to the bartender, "Hey Joe, what's new?"

The bartender replies, "Oh, not much Fred," and jerking his thumb toward the two Irishmen, he adds, "The Murphy twins are drunk again."

A horse walks into a bar and orders a beer

"Coming right up sir," said the bartender.

He pours the beer and as he serves it to the horse he says, "Would you mind if I asked you a question?"

"Go ahead," replied the horse.

The bartender asked, "Why the long face?"

A drunk with a pig under his arm walks into a bar

The bartender looks at the pig and then he asks the drunk, "Where'd you get that thing?"

The pig says, "I won him in a raffle."

Two gorillas are in a bar

They are having a few drinks and one of them says, "Come on man. Just look at that guy over there… his hands… his face. I'm absolutely convinced. We are descended from man!"

A baby seal walks into a bar

… and the bartender asks, "What'll ya have?"

The seal says, "Anything but a Canadian Club."

A reindeer walks into a pub and orders a beer

The bartender serves it up to him and tells him, "That'll be eight dollars please." Then he adds, "You know, we don't see very many reindeer in here."

The reindeer says, "At eight bucks a beer I'm not surprised."

A penguin walks into a bar

…. and asks the bartender, "Have you seen my brother?"

The bartender replies, "I don't know. What does he look like?"

Just how good is Canadian beer?

At the Great Canadian Beer festival, all of the brewery CEOs decided to go out for a beer. They go to a local pub and the pretty beertendress asks for their order.

The guy from Heineken sits down and says, ""Ya you vill please bring to me da finest beer in all da vorld, a Heineken."

The guy from Budweiser says, "Just bring me the king of beers please; a Budweiser."

The guy from Corona says, "Senorita, please bring me the finest beer in all the world; a Corona."

The guy from Steam Whistle says, "I'll just have a Coke please."

Surprised by his request, the other brewery presidents look at him and ask, "Why aren't you having a Steam Whistle beer?"

The president of Steam Whistle says, "Well, I just figured that if you guys weren't going to be drinking beer, neither would I."

The depressed drinker

A guy sits down at the bar and starts ordering beer after beer and chugging them down. After six or seven beers, the bartender asks, "Hey buddy. You're puttin' em away pretty fast there. Everything okay?"

The guy says, "Aw the wife and I had a fight and she said she wasn't going to speak to me for a month."

The bartender says, "Sorry to hear about that."

The guy says, "Yeah… the month is up today."

A really bad day

A little guy is sitting at the bar just staring at his drink when this big, tough, road-worn biker sits down beside him, grabs his drink and gulps it down in one swig. Then he stares menacingly at the little guy as if to say, 'What are y'a gonna do about it?'

The poor little guy starts crying.

The biker is caught off guard by this and feels sorry for him, "Hey man, I was just fooling around. I didn't mean to hurt your feelings. Please don't cry. I can't stand to see a grown man cry."

The little guy sobs as he tells him, "I can't help it. This is absolutely the very worst day of my life. I can't do anything right. I overslept and was late to an important meeting, so my boss fired me. When I went to the parking lot, I found my car was stolen and I don't have any insurance. I left my wallet in the cab I took home. When I got there, I found my wife in bed with the gardener and then to top it all off… my dog bit me!

After all that, I came to this bar trying to work up the courage to put an end to my miserable life and the next thing I know… you show up and drink my poison!"

Why did God give us alcohol?

To keep the Irish from running the world.

Quitting when you're ahead

A guy with a shopping bag walks into a bar. He sets the shopping bag up on the bar, reaches into it and pulls out a live human head which he gently places on the bar. The head smiles at the bartender as the guy says, "Gimme two scotches please – one for me and one for my friend the head here."

The bartender looks at the head in disbelief as the head smiles back at him and says, "Not too much ice please."

After the bartender serves up the two scotches, the man drinks his then grabs the head by the hair, tilts him backward and pours the scotch into the head's open mouth. The head downs it in one gulp.

After doing this, the head the head suddenly sprouts a torso.

The head's buddy says, "Two more scotches please."

The shocked bartender serves them up and after the head downs his second shot, he sprouts two arms.

Now the head's buddy orders two more scotches and this time the head uses his two arms to pick up his scotch and gulp it down. Then he sprouts two legs.

Standing up all by himself now, the head sets his empty glass on the counter and says, "Two more scotches please."

The stunned bartender serves them up and the head–now a fully grown person–reaches for his and gulps it down. Then he convulses in a violent spasm and falls over backward on the floor… dead!

The bartender leans out over the bar and looks down at the guy – lying down there on the floor dead like that – and suddenly he starts laughing.

The head's buddy is shocked and he says to the bartender, "What the heck is so darned funny?"

The bartender, still laughing, says, "He should have quit while he was a head!"

Rubber or plastic?

This loud mouthed, know-it-all jerk, named Ralph, goes into a commuter bar at the subway station. He orders a drink and then, since the bar is quite crowded, takes it to one of those small, round stand-up tables in a corner.

There is one other person at the table. He's very drunk and he's staring intently at something that he's rolling in between his thumb and his forefinger while muttering aloud, "Holy mackerel! Look at thith thing. It lookth like plathtic, but it feelth jutht like rubber."

Ralph rudely grabs the object from the drunk, telling him, "Here, let me have a look at that."

He holds it up to the light and examines it as he rolls it between his thumb and his forefinger.

A few minutes later, he hands it back to the drunk, telling him, "You're right. It does look like plastic and it does feel like rubber. Where did you get it?"

The drunk, suddenly a little less drunk, looks at Ralph, smiles and says, "Out of my nose."

The world's fastest turtle

A guy comes walking into a bar with a little turtle in his hand. The turtle's one eye is black and blue, two of his legs are bandaged, and his whole shell is taped together with duct tape.

The bartender asks the man, "What's wrong with your turtle?"

"Not a thing," the man says. "You my friend are looking at a very fast turtle... in fact he just happens to be the world's fastest turtle."

"Really. How fast is he?" the bartender asks.

The guy points to a dog over in the corner and says, "He's faster than that dog you've got there... a lot faster."

The bartender says, "Yeah... right. I don't think so. That happens to be a purebred greyhound. He's very fast.

The guy says, "I'll tell you what... why don't you take your *very fast* dog and let him stand at this end of the bar. Then you go and stand at the other end of the room and call your dog.

I'll bet you five hundred dollars that before your dog reaches you, my turtle will be there."

The bartender, thinking it's an easy five hundred dollars, agrees. He goes to the other side of the bar, and on the count of three calls his dog. Suddenly the guy picks up his turtle and throws it across the room… narrowly missing the bartender, and smashing into the wall.

Then he turns to the bartender and with a big smile, he says, "You owe me five hundred dollars."

Where do you think Johnny learned to spell?

Asked by his third-grade teacher to spell the word "straight," Johnny did so without error.

"Very good Johnny," said the teacher. "Now, please tell the class what that word means."

Johnny replied, "No water, just a little ice."

You know you've had too much to drink when…

1: You tell your wife, "Don't have anything more to drink dear. Your face is starting to look blurry."

2: Your wife tells you, "Stop telling I look like your first wife stupid. I am your first wife!"

3: You tell your girlfriend, "Let's get married!"

Drinking and driving in Ireland

An Irishman who'd had a little too much to drink is driving home from the pub one night. His car is weaving crazily all over the road and as luck would have it, a cop pulls him over.

The cop says to the driver, "And would y'a mind tellin' me just where you have been?"

"Why, I've been to the pub of course," slurs the Irishman.

"Well," says the cop, "it looks like you've had more than just a few to drink this evening."

"I did all right," he says with a smile.

The cop stands up straight and after folding his arms across his chest, says, "Well you didn't happen to notice did you that your wife fell out of the car a few intersections back?"

"She did? Oh, thank heavens," sighs the Irishman. "For a minute there, I thought I'd gone deaf!"

An Irish widower

An Irishman was sitting in a bar, downing them rapidly when the man on the barstool next to him said, "You seem to be having a bit of a party there... anything wrong?"

The Irishman said, "I'm drinking to the memory of my recently deceased wife... a true saint on this earth."

"Oh that's too bad. Here... let me buy you one. Tell me now, what was she like?"

"Well, she went to church every single morning and spent her day studying the Scriptures. She sang hymns and psalms all evening and she filled our house with religious statues and paintings. She even invited priests and nuns to dinner two or three times a week."

"She sounds like an angel," the second man commented, "I suppose the good Lord took her early to have her for Himself."

"No... *He* didn't," the Irishman replied with a contented smile. "I strangled her."

Irish genies

Two Irishmen were in a lifeboat after their ship sank in a storm. After hours of floating aimlessly, one of them spotted an old lamp in the boat.

Secretly hoping that a genie would appear, he rubbed the lamp vigorously and to the amazement of the castaways, a genie did appear. This particular genie, however, stated that he could only deliver one wish, not the standard three. Without giving much thought to the matter the first man blurted out, "Make the entire ocean into beer!"

The genie clapped his hands and immediately the entire sea turned into the finest brew ever sampled by mortals. His work done, the genie vanished.

Only the gentle lapping of beer on the hull broke the stillness as the two men sat and considered their circumstances.

The second one looked disgustedly at the first whose wish had been granted and said, "Nice going you bloody fool! Now we're going to have to pee in the boat!"

An Irish Miracle

An Irish priest is driving down to New York City and gets stopped for speeding in Connecticut. The state trooper smells alcohol on the priest's breath and upon seeing an empty wine bottle on the floor of the car asks, "Father, have you been drinking?"

"Just water," the priest says with his most pious and innocent smile.

The trooper says, "Then perhaps you could explain to me why I small wine?"

The priest picks up the bottle and sniffs it. With a look of shock and amazement he says, "Good Lord! He's done it again!"

The patch

Will and Timothy were driving down the road drinking beer when Timothy, the passenger, said, "Lord thunderin' heavens Will! There's a police roadblock up ahead! We're gonna get busted!"

"Don't worry, Timothy," Will said. "We just pull over and finish drinkin' these here beers, peel off the labels, stick'em on our foreheads and stash the bottles under the seat. You let me handle it from there."

So, they finished their beers, and then each man peeled off the label and stuck it on his forehead. Next, they stashed the bottles under the seat and slowly drove up to the roadblock.

When they stopped, the cop asked them, "You boys been drinkin'?"

"We most certainly are not, sir", said Will as he pointed to his forehead. "We're on the patch!"

Parkinson's or Alzheimer's

Two men who had just turned seventy were having a couple of scotties and talking about what was left of their future. One of them asked, "At your ripe old age, which disease would you prefer to get – Parkinson's or Alzheimer's?"

Without hesitation, the other man said, "Definitely Parkinson's."
"Why is that?"

"Well, I figure it's better to spill half an ounce of 18 year old Glenfiddich, than to forget where you keep the bottle!"

Cliff Clavin's drinking philosophy

Cliff tells Norm at Cheers, "Ya see, Norm, it's like this... a herd of buffalo can only move as fast as the slowest buffalo. And when the herd is hunted, it is the slowest and weakest ones at the back that are run down and killed first.

This natural selection is good for the herd as a whole, since the general speed and health of the whole group keeps improving by the regular killing of the weakest members.

In much the same way, the human brain can only operate as fast as the slowest brain cells. Excessive intake of alcohol, as we know, kills brain cells. But naturally, it attacks the slowest and weakest brain cells first. In this way, regular consumption of beer eliminates the weaker brain cells, thus making the brain a faster and more efficient machine.

And that my friend is why you always feel smarter after a few beers."

More drinking philosophies…

Ronnie Hawkins

When asked by a reporter what he had done to blow all the money he had earned in his career, 'The Hawk' replied, "Ninety percent of the money I made, I spent on booze, fast cars, drugs and loose women.

The other ten per cent… I wasted."

We drink because…

No great story ever started with a salad.

We drink Scotch because…

One can't solve the world's problems over white wine.

George Burns

"Actually, it only takes one drink to get me loaded. Trouble is… I can't remember if it's the thirteenth or the fourteenth."

Mark Twain

"Sometimes… too much to drink is barely enough."

James Thurber

"One martini is good, two is too many. But three… is not enough."

Hunter S. Thompson

"I hate to advocate drugs, alcohol, violence, or insanity to anyone, but they've always worked for me."

Noel Coward

"I am not a heavy drinker. I can sometimes go for hours without touching a drop."

Al Bundy

"Pretty women make us buy beer. Ugly women make us drink it."

Homer Simpson

"I am in no condition to be driving...wait a minute! I shouldn't be listening to myself... I'm drunk!"

Ben Franklin said it best...

In wine there is wisdom, in beer there is freedom, in water there is bacteria.

W.C. Fields said it funniest

* "It was a woman who drove me to drink and I didn't even have the decency to thank her."

* "Once, during prohibition, I was forced to live for days on nothing but food and water."

* "Always carry a flagon of whiskey in case of snakebite and in case of emergency... always carry a small snake."

* "Everybody's got to believe in something. I believe I'll have another beer."

G.K. Chesterton, *Hercules*

"Drink because we are happy, but never because we are miserable."

The 5 Rules of Alcohol

1. Open bar is a dangerous game. Respect it.
2. Vodka can be mixed with anything... even more vodka.
3. Tequila changes people.
4. If you do something really stupid, never say you are drunk... unless you're not.
5. If she/he's still ugly after the 7th beer, it's time to quit.

Bill Murray

"In alcohol's defense, I've done some pretty dumb stuff while completely sober too."

Chapter 6

Multi-cultural

They have dial-a-prayer for atheists now…

You dial the number. It rings and rings… but nobody answers.

Why did the Canadian cross the road?

To get to the middle.

How do you get 37 people out of a swimming pool in Canada?

You just say, "Okay now… would everybody please get out of the pool."

How Canadians make people crazy

An Englishman, a Canadian and an American were captured and sentenced to be executed by a firing squad. The enemy leader visited them on the eve of their execution and told them, "Before we execute you, you will be allowed to say your last words. Please let me know what you wish to talk about."

With a very stiff upper lip, the Englishman replied, "I wish to speak about loyalty and service to the crown."

The Canadian replied, "I want to talk about the history of an orderly constitutional process in Canada that affords special status within the framework of that constitution. From there I will delve into the notion of a distinct society for the purpose of exploring the general concepts of uniqueness within diversity and from there I will move on to self-rule within the context of institutional continuity."

The American replied, "Please, just make sure you shoot me before that Canadian guy gets started."

A real Canadian bonehead

Some tourists at Toronto's Royal Ontario Museum are marveling at the dinosaur bones. One of them asks the guard, "Can you tell me how old those dinosaur bones are?"

The guard replies, "Those bones right there are sixty five million, four and a half years old."

"That's an awfully exact number," says the tourist. "How do you know their age so precisely?"

The guard answers, "Well, the dinosaur bones were sixty five million years old when I started working here, and that was four and a half years ago."

American vs Canadian fiscal responsibility

When NASA first planned to send up astronauts, they quickly discovered that ball-point pens would not work in zero gravity. To combat the problem, NASA scientists spent a decade and $1.2 billion to develop a pen that writes in zero gravity, upside down, underwater, on almost any surface including glass, and at temperatures ranging from below freezing to +300 C.

Confronted with the same problem, the Canadians used a pencil.

How to get a job in Canada

A young man from Victoria, BC was hired to be the pool lifeguard at the Prime Minister's residence at 24 Sussex Drive. The Harper family was making use of the pool when one of their two children encountered some difficulty and cried for help. The lifeguard ignored the cries, so the Prime Minister himself had to plunge into the pool to rescue the boy.

Afterwards, Harper grilled the lifeguard. "What's the matter with you? Didn't you see that my son was in trouble?"

The lifeguard smiled and told him, "Yes, sir. I did."

"Well then… why didn't you jump in and help him?" the PM asked.

The lifeguarded smugly answered, "That's easy sir. I can't swim."

The Prime Minister was stunned as he said, "You can't swim! How the hell did you ever land a job as a lifeguard?"

With a look of righteous indignation the man puffed his chest out and replied, "That's easy monsieur, I'm bilingual."

The Canadian genie

A Canadian was camping in Algonquin Park when he found an old brass lamp. As he rubbed it to clean it up, a genie appeared and offered him three wishes. The Canadian guy thought for a minute and then said, "Well… the very first thing I want is a bottle of Canadian Club whiskey that never gets empty."

The genie said, "No problem."

He snapped his fingers and 'poof,' there was a 40 ounce bottle of 12 year old Canadian Club Chairman's Select. The Canadian smiled, picked up the bottle along with the lamp and then told the genie, "I think I'll just take the whiskey and go home to think about my next two wishes. Is that okay with you?"

"That's okay by me," said the genie. "Just rub the lamp when you decide what you want."

The Canadian turned out to be very happy with his wish and spent the next two weeks testing his new bottle to its limits. It never let him down: every time he picked the bottle up, it was full to the brim and the quality was superb. He stayed drunk for the next month before he awoke one morning, reached under the bed, pulled out the lamp and summoned his new pal… the genie.

The genie appeared, "Hello again master. You have two more wishes. Have you figured out what you would like?"

The Canadian replied, "Yes I have. Do you remember that wonderful, never ending bottle of Canadian Club Chairman's Select whiskey you gave me for my first wish?"

"Yes master, I most certainly do," the genie replied.

"Well," he said, "I'd like two more of those please."

The Newfoundland state of mind

A Newfoundlander was walking past his neighbor one day with his dog in one hand and a shotgun in the other.

The neighbor asked, "Where you going boy?"

The man said, "To shoot my dog."

The neighbor asked, "Is he mad?"

The man said, "Well… I wouldn't say he was mad but I don't think he's real thrilled about it."

Newfoundland logic

A Hollywood film crew is in Newfoundland filming a documentary on whales. They hired Captain Angus McWalters along with his boat and crew to take them out to whale territory and to assist with the diving scenes using the underwater cameras.

After a tough six-week shooting schedule the director felt that he had all the film he needed. As a way of thanking the captain and his crew for their tireless efforts, he took them all out for dinner. During the dinner the director said to the captain, "Captain Angus, would you mind if I asked you a question?"

"Fire away lad," the captain replied.

"Well sir, every day when you and your crew dove in to the water, you guys would sit up on the side of the boat, hold your hands over those diving masks you wear and then fall backwards into the water. Why did you do it that way?'

Captain Angus looked at the director like he had six heads and said, "Lard thunderin' heavens! You Hollywood lads aren't too frickin' smart when it comes to the sea now are y'a? Can't y'a see lad that if we fell forward, we'd still be in the frickin' boat!"

When the Canadian honeymoon is really over

Alan and Sandra lived on a cove in Atlantic Canada. It was early winter and the lower portion of the cove had frozen over.

One Saturday night about halfway through the hockey game, Alan realized that he only had two beers and five cigarettes left so, not wanting to miss any of the hockey game, he asked Sandra if she would walk across the frozen part of the cove to the general store and get him some smokes and beer.

When she asked him for some money, but he told her, "Nah, just put it on our tab. Old man Stacey won't mind."

So Sandra, being a most excellent Canadian wife, walked across the ice, got the smokes and beer at the store and then walked back home across the cove. When she got home with the items she said, "Alan, you always tell me not to run up the tab at Stacey's store. Why didn't you just give me some money?"

Alan replied, "Well, Sandra, I didn't want to send you out there with cash when I wasn't sure how thick the ice was!"

The major difference between a Canadian and an American

A Canadian not only has a sense of humour, he also knows how to spell it.

How to start a small business in Canada

Start a big one and wait!

The Canadian lottery blues

Two farmers are settin' on the porch one evening during a visit. Their conversation was, as usual about how hard it was to make a buck when you were always dealing with all the government regulations and farm marketing boards. Eventually one of them asked, "What do you think you'd do if you was to wake up tomorrow morning and find out you'd won two million in the lottery?"

The other one replied, "Oh I don't s'pose I'd change too much. I really like bein' a farmer and all so I s'pose I'd just keep on farming 'til the money run out."

How Canadians live longer

A man visiting his doctor is told he has only six months to live. He asks, "Is there anything I can do to help me live longer than that?"

The doctor replies, "Well, you could get married and move to Sudbury, Ontario."

"You're kidding? Just do that and I'll live longer?"

"No you won't. It'll just seem longer."

The great Canadian hobby – Leaf bashing

Aside from the fact that all these teams are from Toronto, what do the Toronto Maple Leafs, Toronto Raptors and the Toronto Blue Jays all have in common?

A: None of them can play hockey.

The great Canadian Johnny joke

The teacher asked her grade six class to make a list with the names of six great Canadians on it. Ten minutes later she noticed that everyone but Johnny had stopped writing.

She asked him, "What's the matter Johnny, can't you think of six great Canadians?"

With an exasperated glare at the teacher, Johnny replied, "I'm working on it okay? I have five, but I still need a goalie."

Canadian hockey moms

At one point during a game, the coach called Mitchell, one of his eight-year old hockey players aside and asked, "Mitchell, do you understand what cooperation is? What team-play is really all about?"

Mitchell nodded his head slowly in the affirmative.

"That's good," the coach replied. "Now then, do you understand that what really matters here is not whether we win or lose but how we come together to play as a team?"

Again young Mitchell nodded solemnly in complete agreement.

"So," the coach continued, "I'm sure you know that when a penalty is called, you shouldn't argue, curse, attack the referee, or call him a dick-head. Do you understand that?"

Again young Mitchell nodded.

The coach was on a roll now as he continued, "And when I take you out of the game so that another boy can have a chance to play, do you agree that it's not good sportsmanship to call your coach a 'door knob'?"

Mitchell replied, "Yes coach... I sure do."

"Good," said the coach. "Now would you mind going over and explaining all that to your mother."

A great Canadian nails it

Dave Broadfoot at Montreal's Just For Laughs festival:

* "In Canada, you can't vote if you're insane, but... you can get elected!"

* "The main difference between Canadians and Americans is that in a recent election in Iowa, only 10% of the voters even turned out while in a recent election in Quebec, 110% of the voters turned out."

The Canadian farmer

A Canadian who owned a small farm in Saskatchewan was being interviewed by a Ministry of Labor Relations official who was checking to see if was paying proper wages to his staff.

"I need to see a list of your employees and your payroll records," demanded the official.

"Well," replied the farmer, "there's my farm hand. He's been with us for three years. I pay him two hundred and fifty dollars a week plus he gets free room and board.

There's the cook/housekeeper. She's been with us for eighteen months, and we pay her three hundred dollars a week and she also gets free room and board.

"Then there's the half-wit. That poor son-of-a-bitch works about eighteen hours every day and he does about ninety per cent of all the work around here. He makes about a hundred and sixty five dollars a week and he pays his own room and board.

I buy him a case of beer every Saturday night. He also sleeps with my wife occasionally."

The agent says, "That's the guy I want to talk to...the half-wit."

"That would be me," replied the farmer.

How a Canadian plans ahead

He buys two cases of beer.

Smart guys from Saskatchewan

You can never underestimate the innovative genius of Saskatchewan farm boys. At a high school in the small town of Wadena, a group of farm boy students decided to play a prank. They let three goats run loose inside the school during school hours. Before turning them loose, they painted numbers on the sides of the goats: 1, 2 and 4.

School Administrators spent most of the day looking for... goat number 3.

Airline service?

A man is sitting alone in an airport lounge when a beautiful woman walks in and sits down at the table next to him. He decides, because she's wearing a uniform, she's probably an off-duty flight attendant. Motivated by this deduction he decides to have a go at picking her up by identifying the airline she flies with, thus impressing her greatly.

For his first attempt, he leans across to her and in his sexiest voice, whispers the British Airways motto, "To Fly... To Serve?"

The woman looks at him blankly.

Undaunted, he sits back, recalls another line and again leans forward again to deliver the Air France motto, "Winning the hearts of the world!"

She just turns and stares at him with a slightly puzzled look on her face.

He decides to try one more. This time he says the Malaysian Airlines motto, "Going beyond expectations!"

The woman looks at him and asks, "What the hell do you want?"

"Aha!" he says, "Air Canada!"

Helpful Canadians

A man traveling by train in British Columbia asked the ticket collector what time the train stopped at Victoria. The conductor replied, "Sir, this train doesn't stop at Victoria."

Startled to hear this, the man told him, "But I have to get off this train in Victoria!"

The conductor patiently explained, "I'm very sorry sir, but this train does not and therefore, will not stop at Victoria."

The guy pleaded with him, "You don't understand. I have a very important meeting in Victoria. I must get off there!"

The conductor mulled it over for a few seconds and then said, "Well, there might be a way I could help you. I might be able to get the engineer to slow down the train a little. Then I can grab you by the scruff of your collar, dangle you out the door and lower you onto the platform."

The man agreed, "That's fine. I am desperate to get off this train in Victoria so I'll try anything."

As they approached the Victoria platform, the train began slowing from fifty miles an hour to thirty miles per hour. The conductor grabbed the man by the scruff of the collar, hung him out the door and the guy started running in mid-air.

The conductor told him, "Cummon man! Run! Faster! Faster!"

With that he started to lower the man until his feet touched the platform. The guy's legs were a blur as he air-ran to get them moving at the same speed as the train slowed a little more. His legs spun faster until he got them in sync with the train speed and the ground. When the conductor let go, the guy hit the ground at twenty five miles an hour and started to slow down. He'd made it!

The other passengers stared in amazement.

But... just as the last car went by, a hand reached out and grabbed the man by the scruff of his collar and lifted him right back onto the train!

As the guy stood there, unable to believe what had just taken place, the gent who picked him up said, "Man you're lucky I was here to help you get on the train! This train doesn't stop in Victoria!"

The great Canadian moose hunters

Stan and Wally drive from Hamilton up to Timmins, Ontario where they hire a twin engine float plane to fly them north into the Canadian bush for three days of moose hunting.

Three days later the pilot returns to pick them up and asks them how the hunting was.

"Great," says Stan. "We've got six moose to take back with us."

The pilot replies, "Six moose! I'll never be able to strap six moose on this plane and then fly us all out of here."

"Why not?" Wally asks. "We did it last year."

"It's just way too heavy a load," the pilot replied. "It would be very dangerous to try and fly this plane out of here with that kind of weight on it."

Stan steps in and says, "Come on man. Last year our pilot had the same plane you do and we just paid him an extra $200 for the added weight. We'll gladly do the same for you."

The pilot reluctantly accepts the deal saying, "Okay. For an extra two hundred dollars I'll give it a shot."

So they strap all six moose onto the plane, get aboard, taxi right down to the very end of the lake and take off.

They barely get the plane up high enough to clear the treetops at the other end of the lake but unfortunately, the surrounding mountains prove too much for the overloaded plane to fly over and they crash in the forest.

Luckily, they all managed to crawl out of the flaming wreck to safety after which Wally asked Stan, "Where do you think we are?"

Stan does a quick visual survey of their surroundings and replies, "Looks to me like we're right about the same place we crashed last year."

Canadian Naval sensitivity

Captain James of the Royal Canadian Navy Minesweeper, H.M.C.S. Meritonia, received a dispatch with the message: "Please inform First Class Seaman Mumford that his mother has passed away."

The Captain called in the Chief Petty Officer, a rather gruff-looking individual and handed him the dispatch – telling him to, "Look after this."

"Aye, Aye sir," said the CPO.

He left the Captain's quarters, went down to the radio room, got on the intercom and proceeded to announce, "Now hear this! Now hear this! First Class Seaman Mumford… your mother's dead!"

When the Captain heard the CPOs' announcement he was flabbergasted and summoned the CPO to his quarters, "On the double!"

When the CPO arrived, the angry captain admonished him saying,

"What the hell were you thinking? You can't give that kind of news to somebody that way. We are responsible for the safety and well-being of these men. A situation like this requires tact and discretion. Next time, use your bloody head and exercise some diplomacy!"

"Aye, Aye sir," said the CPO.

Two weeks later, the Captain gets another dispatch: "Please inform First Class Seaman Mumford that his father has just passed away."

The Captain summoned the CPO to his quarters, handed him the notice and said, "Now this time, I want you to handle this situation tactfully. Any screw-ups and I'll have you busted so low, you'll be saluting civilians! Understood?"

"Aye, Aye sir," replied the CPO and headed down to the radio room where he proceeded to announce over the intercom: "Now hear this! Now hear this! I want all first class seamen assembled on the foredeck in fifteen minutes."

Fifteen minutes later, all the First Class Seamen were assembled on the foredeck and standing smartly at attention.

The CPO addressed them: "At ease men. Now then… I want all first class seamen whose fathers are still living to take one step forward."

Then the CPO pointed at Mumford and bellowed, "Not so fast there Mumford!"

What comes after two days of rain in British Columbia?

Five more days of rain.

A fast thinking guy from Newfoundland

An American and a Newfie go into a pastry shop. The American guy whisks three cookies into his pocket with lightning speed – so fast that the baker doesn't notice.

The American guy then turns to the Newfie and with a smug look says, "You see how clever we are? You Newfies can never beat that!"

The Newfie says to the American guy, "Watch this laddie. You're about to learn a valuable lesson from the master."

He tells the baker, "Give me three of those cookies and I'll show you a magic trick!"

The baker is suspicious but the Newfie says, "Don't worry son, I'll give you five dollars for them if you're not impressed."

The baker gives him the cookies, which the Newfie promptly eats and then stands there with a big smile on his face.

The baker is a little impatient as he asks him, "Okay! Where is this famous magic trick of yours?"

The Newfie says, "Alright then…. now…" With a flourish he points to the American guy's pocket and says, "Abra kadabra!"

Now he turns to the baker and says, "Okay now… take a look in my American friend's pocket!"

Ontario wolves and Newfoundland wolves

The head of the Ontario Fisheries and Wildlife Department called the head of the Newfoundland Fisheries and Wildlife department and told him, "I'm calling you to inform you that we've captured a Newfoundland wolf here in Ontario."

The Newfoundland Wildlife guy said, "Well tanks fer callin' but how do ye' know de wolf is from Newfoundland?"

The Ontario Wildlife guy says, "Because it got caught in one of our traps, chewed off three of its legs and it's still caught in the trap!"

A fish story

On his way home, with the fish he has caught that day slung over his shoulder on a stringer, Dave meets Ned, one of his buddies who asks him, "Hey Dave! How was the fishing?"

Dave says, "Oh, not too bad."

Ned says, "I tell you what… if I can guess how many fish you caught, will you give me one?"

Dave smiles and says, "Heck, if you can tell me exactly how many fish I caught, I'll give them both to you."

The test

Tattersall and Skinner apply for an engineering position at a chemical plant in Sarnia, Ontario's Chemical Valley. Since they both had a Chemical Engineering degree from Queen's University, they were given a test by the plant manager.

After reviewing the tests, both men had only missed one of the questions and the manager went to Skinner and said, "Thank you for your interest, but we've decided to give the job to Mr. Tattersall."

Skinner said, "Why would you do that? We both got 9 questions correct and with this being Sarnia and me being a native Sarnian and

Tattersall being from Toronto, I thought I would get the job!"

The manager said, "Well… under normal circumstances that's how it would have gone but we made our decision not on the correct answers, but on the question you missed."

Skinner said, "And just how would one incorrect answer be better than the other?"

The manager replied, "Simple. On question #5 Mr. Tattersall put down, 'I don't know.' You put down 'Neither do I.'"

Coast guarding

It's 2 am and a Winnipeg man and his wife are asleep when the phone rings. The guy answers it and his wife wakes in time to hear him say, "How the hell should I know stupid. We're in the middle of the prairies." Then he slams the phone down.

His wife asks him, "Who was that?"

He tells her, "Aw, it was just some idiot from the Coast Guard."

She says, "The Coast Guard? How do you know that?"

He tells her, "He wanted to know if the coast was clear."

Your basic Canadian blonde

A blonde calls Air Canada and asks, "Can you please tell me how long it will take to fly non-stop from Toronto to Fort Lauderdale?"

The agent says, "Just a minute please…"

The blonde says, "Thank you," and hangs up.

A Canadian blonde waitresses

In a coffee shop in Fort McMurray, a man tells a blonde waitress, "I'd like a cup of coffee please… with no cream and no sugar."

With a smile, she tells him, "I'm sorry but you'll have to have it with no sugar. We're out of cream."

Canadian logic

Frank and Larry drive from Alberta to British Columbia on a one week salmon fishing trip. They buy all the equipment: the reels, rods and lures. When they get there they stay at a fishing lodge and rent a boat. The trip literally costs them a fortune.

The first day they go fishing, but they don't catch anything. The same thing happens on the second day, and then again on the third day. It goes on like this until finally, on the last day of their vacation,

Larry catches a Sockeye Salmon.

Driving home, they're really depressed at their lousy luck. Frank turns to Larry and says, "Do you realize that one lousy fish we caught cost us thirty six hundred dollars?"

Frank tells him, "No kidding?!" He thinks about that for a minute and then adds, "Man… it's a good thing we didn't catch any more!"

Speaking Canadian

While travelling by train across Canada, an American couple stepped off the train onto the platform to stretch their legs during a stop. The man asked one of the locals nearby, "What town is this?"

"Saskatoon, Saskatchewan," came the reply.

The man's wife said, "Why don't you ask this next gentleman, dear? Perhaps he speaks English."

What's in a name?

A guy from Tobermory, Ontario drives all the way to Toronto in order to enter a petition in court to have his name legally changed.

The judge says, "I see here that your name is Marvin Wienerhead and that you would like to have it changed. Is that correct?"

The man replies, "Yes it is your honour."

The judge says, "Well Mr. Wienerhead, that is not going to be a problem. I can certainly understand why you would want to have that name changed. Now what would you like to have it changed to?"

The man says, "Melvin Wienerhead."

The meaning of "chutzpah"

Chutzpah is a Yiddish word meaning gall, brazen nerve; basically sheer guts plus a touch of arrogance; it's Yiddish and, as Yiddish humorist Leo Rosten writes, no other word and no other language can do it justice. Here's an example that describes it perfectly:

A little old lady sold pretzels on a street corner for a dollar each. Every day a young man would leave his office building at lunch time and as he passed the pretzel stand, he would leave her a dollar… but he never took a pretzel.

This offering went on for more than three years and during that time, the two of them never spoke… not a word.

One day as the young man passed the old lady's stand and left his usual dollar, the pretzel lady spoke to him for the first time in over three years.

Without blinking an eye she looked at him and said, "They're a dollar and a quarter now."

A very clever guy named Sidney

Sidney Mendlebaum is in New York City's Greenwich Village, where he visits an old gypsy fortuneteller: Madam Zelda. She convinces Sidney that for the small fee of $500, she can put him in touch with his long-dead mother. He forks over the money, and Madam Zelda leans across the table in the dimly-lit room, saying - "You vill close your eyes undt join handts vit me, vile I summon za spirit uf your long deadt mother."

After a few moments of Madame Zelda's chanting, Sidney hears a distant voice saying, "Sidney, – Sidney Mendlebaum, are you there? Sidney, Sidney – this is your mama, can you hear me?"

"Mama! This is your son Sidney, Where are you?"

"Oy, Sidney, I'm in heaven. It's luffly here. Listen… Sidney. I can't stay long; I got a MahJong game vit zum uf mine friends. You got anyt'ing you vant you should ask me?"

Sidney leans forward and says, "Yes mama, I've got one question. Where did you learn to speak English?"

The difference between a schmuck and a putz

A schmuck is a guy who falls off the 30th floor balcony.

A putz is the guy he lands on.

What is a "schmuck"

Sadie says to her husband Manny, "You know Manny, you are a real schmuck! You are the biggest schmuck I've ever met in my life. In fact, if they had a contest to see who the biggest schmuck in the world was, you would come in second."

Manny replies, "Vat? Only second! Vy wouldn't I come in foist?"

Sadie replies, "Because Manny… you're a schmuck!"

Don't get mad, get even

Manny is on his deathbed at Cedars of Lebanon Hospital and he calls his lifelong pal and business partner, Sol, to his bedside.

"Solly, I can't leave this world without telling you what a rotten business partner and terrible friend I've been to you. I embezzled over a million dollars from the company and made another million by selling company secrets to the competition. To be spiteful, I fired the receptionist because I knew she was in love with you and then I had an affair with your wife for five years."

"That's all right Manny," Solly replied as he leaned in closer and whispered to him, "Manny my old friend, I don't want you should concern yourself with such things. Instead I want you should concern yourself with this. I'm the one who poisoned you."

Integrity

Irving's son Manny asks him one day, "Papa, what is integrity?"

Irving thinks for a moment and then says, "That's a very difficult word to define my son, so perhaps I could best explain integrity to you by giving you an example.

Yesterday morning, Mrs. Jones bought something in our store for $99.50 and paid for it with a brand new $100 dollar bill. As I reached into the till to get her fifty cents change, I realized that she had, by mistake, given me two new $100 bills which had stuck together.

Now then... integrity is this... should I tell my partner?"

Looking for love in all the wrong places

During afternoon tea at a swanky resort in the Catskills, Sylvia spies an older man sitting by the pool drinking his tea... all by himself. She is interested what with her being recently widowed and on the make so... she saunters over to him and introduces herself. He introduces himself as Manny.

Sylvia says, "Oy Manny... you're such a gorgeous man. Why is it that I haven't seen you around here before?"

Manny tells her, "Well Sylvia, the reason you haven't seen me here before is that I was in prison for the last thirty years."

Sylvia was shocked, "In prison for thirty years! My god, Manny! What did you do that you should be locked up in prison for thirty years?"

Manny looked at her with icy cold eyes and calmly told her, "I murdered my unfaithful wife and her boyfriend."

Sylvia is horrified as she says, "I can't believe it. You actually murdered them?"

Sydney says, "Yes I did Sylvia. I took an axe and chopped them both into a hundred bloody pieces, and for this I got thirty years in prison."

Gathering her composure and showing him her sweetest smile, Sylvia says, "So… you're single?"

A real Polish joke

A Polish guy is at the eye doctor having his eyes examined. He is looking at the eye chart as the doctor asks him, "Can you read that?"

The Polish guy replied, "Read it. Heck, the guy on the fourth line is my brother-in-law!"

The travel agency

A guy walks into a travel agency and asks for the agency's special Hawaiian tour. The travel agent takes his deposit and asks him to fill out some forms in the office next door and when he goes into the room, somebody whacks him over the head and knocks him out.

Later that day, another guy walks into the same travel agency and asks for the same special Hawaiian tour. Again the agent takes his deposit and sends him next door to fill out the special forms. He also gets whacked on the head and knocked out.

When the two guys wake up, they find themselves floating in the ocean, about ten miles off Oahu in a small rubber dinghy.

One of them looks at the other and asks, "I wonder if they'll fly us back home?"

The other one says, "I don't think they will. They didn't last year."

The Italian astronaut program

An American is on a tour of Italy. In the bar of his hotel in Rome, he winds up talking to a local man who starts coming down on Americans in general because, "You people thinka that everything you a do is a de best ting ever!"

The American replies, "Well I think you have to admit that the USA has some very significant and important accomplishments in the last century. For instance we were the first to fly in 1903 and sixty four years later we put a man on the moon."

The Italian guy says, "Oh man… that's a nothing. Italy is a-gonna put a man on the sun."

The American says, "Don't be ridiculous. You can't fly to the sun. It's too hot. Your space ship will burn up."

The Italian guy says, "What's - a- mata for you? You thinka we crazy or some-a-ting? We know-a-that. That's-a-why we gonna go at night!"

The Irish Sugar Test

Old Muldoon goes into a pharmacy, reaches into his pocket and takes out a small bottle and a teaspoon. He sets them up on the counter and asks Killoran, the pharmacist, "Would you mind tasting this for me, please."

Since Killoran had known Muldoon all his life, he went along with the request. He took the spoon and poured a tiny dab of the liquid on it then he put it in his mouth. He swilled the liquid around and then spit it out into a cup.

"Now does that taste sweet to you?" Muldoon asked.

The pharmacist said, "No Muldoon. It certainly does not!"

"Oh that's a relief," says Muldoon.

"Why is that?" Killoran asked.

Muldoon replied, "Well… the doctor told me to come over here and get my urine tested for sugar."

Wheeler dealers

Manny and Solly, two retired businessmen meet for lunch in Miami. Manny says, "Solly my old friend, today is your lucky day. Have I got a deal for you! When I was over on the east coast, I went to the town where the circus stays during the winter. It was there that I happened to pick up some elephants at a fantastic price. I could let you have one for… say… a thousand dollars."

Solly replies, "What are you, crazy? What am I going to do with an elephant? I live in a condo. I barely have room for my furniture. I can't even squeeze in an end table. So now I'm going to buy an elephant?"

Manny says, "Okay then… I could let you have three of them for two grand."

Solly smiles and says, "Now we're talking!"

Native American cusswords

A Cherokee Indian was a special guest at an inner-city elementary school. He was there to talk to the children about his tribe and its traditions. At the end of his presentation he shared with them this interesting fact: "There are no swear words in the Cherokee language."

One boy raised his hand, "But what if you're hammering a nail and accidentally smash your thumb?"

"That," the man answered, "is when we use your language."

Irish death notice

Gallagher opened the morning newspaper and was dumbfounded to read in the obituary column that he had died.

He quickly phoned his best friend, Finney. "Did you see the paper?" asked Gallagher. "They say I've died!!"

"Yes, I saw it!" replied Finney. "Where are ye callin' from?"

Irish logic

A man in a hot air balloon is lost over Ireland. He looks down and sees a farmer in the fields and shouts down to him, "Where am I?"

The Irish farmer looks back up and shouts back. "You can't fool me. You're in that basket up there."

The church of what's happening now

The elderly priest, speaking to the younger priest, said, "Father, I want to congratulate you on your excellent suggestion to replace the first four pews with plush bucket theater seats. It worked like a charm. The front of the church always fills first now."

The young priest nodded as the old priest continued, "And you told me that adding a little more beat to the music would bring young people back to church, so I'm glad I supported you when you brought in that rock'n'roll gospel choir. Now our services are consistently packed to the balcony."

"Thank you, Father," answered the young priest. "I'm glad they worked and that that you are open to these new ideas of today"

"All of these new ideas of yours have been well and good," said the elderly priest, "but I'm afraid you've gone too far with this drive-thru confessional thing."

"But, Father," protested the young priest, "my confessions and the donations have nearly doubled since I began that!"

"Yes I know," replied the elderly priest, "and I appreciate that. But the Bishop insists that the flashing neon sign, 'Toot 'n Tell or Go to Hell' cannot stay on the church roof."

Nazi archeology

A Nazi archaeological expedition discovered an ancient tomb in Egypt. Inside they discovered a mummy. What a great achievement for the Third Reich! How proud the Fuhrer would be.

Realizing that the discovery would not be recognized by the international archaeological community unless they could accurately date the mummy, the big question was; which branch of the Nazi administration should the mummy be turned over to for official dating determination?

The decision was made when one of those weird, monocle-wearing, evil-looking dorks in a black leather trench-coat from the dreaded S.S., claimed that the S.S. was the branch most capable of determining the exact age of the mummy.

No one dared to argue with him.

Exactly eighteen hours later, the S.S. reported that the exact age of the mummy was 3,364 years.

"Zat iss amazing," the other Nazis said. "How did you make zose calculations so quickly?"

"Zimple," said the S.S. agent, "He confessed!"

Beware the Scottish immigrant

There was a young Scottish lad named Angus who decided to try life in Australia. He went 'down under,' found an apartment in a small building and settled in.

After a week or two, his mother called from Aberdeen to inquire as to how her son was doing in his new life.

"I'm fine," Angus said, "But there are some really strange people living here in Australia. One woman cries all day long, another lies on her floor moaning, and there is a guy next door to me who bangs his head on the wall all the time."

"Well, ma wee laddie," says his mother, "I suggest you dunna associate with people like that."

"Oh," says Angus, "I don't, Ma'am, I don't. No, I just stay inside ma apartment all day and night, playin' ma bagpipes."

How the Irish handle the religion thing

An Irish guy walking along a railroad track stumbles and gets his foot caught in the track. He tries hard to get it out but to no avail; it was really stuck. Hearing a noise behind him, he turns around and is shocked to see a train coming.

In a panic mode he starts to pray, "Dear God, please get my foot out of these tracks and I'll stop drinking!"

Alas… nothing happened: his foot was still stuck, and the train was getting closer!

He prayed again, "God, please get my foot free and I'll stop drinking and cussing!"

Still nothing and now the train was just seconds away!

Again he prayed, "Oh God please, if you get my foot out of the tracks, I'll quit drinking, cussing, smoking and fooling around with married women."

Suddenly his foot came free and he was able to dive out of the way of the oncoming train… just in the nick of time.

He got up, dusted himself off, raised his eyes toward heaven and said, "Thanks for listening… but I got it myself."

A true Irish tragedy

Brenda O'Malley is home making dinner, as usual, when Tim Finnegan arrives at her door.

"Brenda, may I please come in for a moment?" he asks. "I've somethin' to tell ya."

Brenda smiles as she opens the door, "Of course you can come in. You're always welcome here Tim. But where's my husband Shamus?"

"That's what I'm here to be telling ya about Brenda. There was an accident down at the Guinness brewery…"

"Oh, Lord no!" cries Brenda. "Please don't tell me…"

Tim shakes his head slowly, "Sadly, that is what I must do Brenda. Your poor husband Shamus is dead and gone and for that I want you to know, I am truly sorry."

She was silent for a moment. Finally, she asked, "That's terrible, terrible news Tim. How did it happen?"

"It was a tragic and unfortunate thing Brenda. The poor man fell into a vat of Guinness Stout… and drowned."

"Now please tell me true Tim that at least he did go quickly?"

"Well, Brenda… sadly he did not. In fact, the poor man got out three times just to pee."

Irish healthcare

Mrs. McRee is not too pleased with her doctor. He has been prescribing various, costly medicines to cure her cold and none of them are working.

"Sure and what is it ye are going to waste me money on today?" she asked.

The doctor replied, "Go home, take a cold shower and stand outside naked in a draft until ye're thoroughly dry."

"And ye're sayin' that'll cure me?" she asked.

"Don't be ridiculous! There's no frickin' way it'll cure ye'! It'll give you pneumonia. But I can cure that!"

What men do for love

A woman on vacation in Kelowna, British Columbia went for an early morning walk on a trail beside a beautiful lake. Along the trail she met a Native Canadian who was standing on the shore watching the sunrise. After telling him what a beautiful lake it was, she asked him the name of it.

He replied, "My forefathers named this lake many years ago in memory of a young brave who was a member of our tribe. In those days we were at war with the tribe who lived across the lake from us. This young brave from our tribe fell in love with a beautiful maiden from that tribe across the lake.

Since our tribes were at war, they were forbidden to see each other. But, as young lovers will, they would often sneak away to be with each other.

During the summer, the young brave would swim across the lake, which took about half an hour. But in the winter, the water was too cold and dangerous for swimming, so he would have to walk around the lake, which took about three hours.

One spring, even though the water was still too cold for swimming, he decided to save time and tried to swim across the icy, cold lake anyway. Alas, he was never seen or heard from again.

As our way of remembering this young brave, my people named this lake in honour of him."

Again she asked, "So then, what is the name of the lake?"

He replied, "We call it Lake Stupid."

The Amish go green

Sign on the back of a Pennsylvania Amish horse-drawn carriage:

Caution!

Energy efficient vehicle: runs on oats and grass.

Be careful not to step in exhaust.

Ronald Reagan's Russian joke

A man in Russia has finally saved up enough money to buy a car and goes to his local dealer to put one on order. He is told that there is a ten year wait to get a new car and his name will be put on a list.

He agrees and pays for the car. Then he is told that the car will be delivered exactly ten years from that day.

He tells the car dealer, "Okay comrade but it will have to be in the afternoon."

The car dealer asks him, "What difference does it make whether it's afternoon or morning? It's ten years from now!"

The guy tells him, "Well… the plumber is coming in the morning."

Heard about the Polish lottery?

If you win, you get $10 a year for a million years.

A Jewish holiday

During his reign of terror, Adolph Hitler used any means possible to improve his chances for success at holding on to his power. This included astrology. The finest astrologer he could find was a Jewish fellow, so he put aside his prejudice in the interest of personal gain and consulted the Jewish astrologer at every turn: battle plans, political strategy, etc.

One day, Hitler became quite curious about the day his reign may or may not come to an end. More specifically, he wanted to know about his death so, he consulted his trusted astrologer.

"Can you tell when I'm going to die?" he asked.

"That's a little difficult," replied the astrologer. "But, what I can tell you is that your death will occur on a Jewish holiday."

"Really?" Hitler was fascinated and he asked, "Which one?"

His astrologer replied with an even tone, "I don't know exactly what day Mein Fuhrer, but I think it's fair to say that any day you die is definitely going to be a Jewish Holiday."

Fast-thinking enemies

A newly enlisted Israeli soldier, asked his Commanding Officer for a three-day pass. The CO said, "Now let me get this straight. You just joined the Israeli army yesterday and already you are asking for a three-day pass? No way! You have to do something really spectacular for that kind of recognition!"

The very next day, the soldier came back driving an Arab tank! The CO was very impressed and the soldier got his three-day pass.

One of the other new recruits took him aside and asked him how he had managed to single-handedly capture an Arab tank.

"Simple," said the soldier. "I jumped in one of our tanks and headed towards the border. As I approached the border, I saw an Arab tank. I put my white flag up and the Arab tank put his white flag up.

We pulled our tanks up beside each other and I asked the Arab soldier, 'How would you like to get a three-day pass?'

He said, 'Great!'

So we exchanged tanks!"

Irish Catholics vs. the English

A young Irish priest was stationed at a parish in New York City. During his sermons, he liked to take as many shots at the English as he could and he was constantly referring to, "those potato-thievin' English!"

Eventually, some of the wealthier, pro-English parishioners complained about this to the Bishop who subsequently summoned the young priest to his office. In a very firm manner, he laid down the law and ordered the young priest not to say anything at all derogatory about the English in any of his future sermons since it was affecting the welfare of the parish… namely, the collection plate.

The young priest reluctantly complied, but deep down, he still bore a mighty resentment for the English.

On Good Friday, the young priest was telling the faithful the story of the Last Supper. Finally, he came to the part where Jesus said; "Tonight one of you will betray me thrice." The young priest continued, "Peter was the first to approach Jesus, asking, 'Is it I Lord?' and Jesus told him, 'No Peter, it is not you.'

Then Mathew, John and Luke each approached Jesus with the same question, and were all given the same answer. 'No, it is not you.'

Finally Judas, the apostle who actually betrayed him, approached Jesus and asked, 'Oi say guv'nor. Is it Oi?'"

A Palestinian/Israeli point of view

At a United Nations Assembly, a representative from Israel came to the podium and said, "Before beginning my talk, I want to tell an interesting story about Moses. When he struck the rock and it brought forth water, he thought, 'What a perfect opportunity to take a bath!'

He removed his clothes, put them aside and entered the water. When he came out and wanted to get dressed, he was shocked to discover that his clothes had vanished. This was because a Palestinian had stolen them."

The Palestinian representative jumped up angrily and shouted, "What are you talking about? There's no way a Palestinian could have done that. The Palestinians weren't even there then!"

The Israeli representative nodded in agreement to the Palestinian. Then he turned to face the rest of the assembly, smiled and said, "And now that we are all in agreement on that point, I would like to begin my speech…"

Texas warning sign

Do not cross this pasture unless you can do it in 9 seconds, because there's a bull in here that can do it in 10.

You gotta know when your prayer is being answered

During a particularly wet Arkansas spring, floodwaters rise so high in one town that the National Guard is called in to evacuate all the residents. Zeke stays behind, however, and when the water is waist-high, two national guardsmen in a motorboat pass his house; checking for people left behind.

They tell him, "We're evacuating the town because of the flood! Jump in the boat and we'll carry you to safety!"

But Zeke says, "No, don't bother. I've led a very pious life, and I have faith that the Lord will save me."

The men in the boat shrug their shoulders and motor away.

Later, when the water level has driven Zeke onto his roof, another boat appears. They tell Zeke, "Haven't you heard? The town has been evacuated? Come on. Get in the boat and we'll save you!"

But Zeke sends them away again, saying, "No, no. Please don't worry. I have faith that the Lord will save me!"

The water level keeps rising until finally, Zeke is standing on his chimney and barely keeping his head above water. A helicopter, doing a final check, appears overhead. It drops a rope down, and a loudspeaker from the chopper says, "Grab the rope and we'll bring you to safety!"

But Zeke waves the helicopter away, once again saying, "No, no. The Lord will save me!"

But the water level keeps rising, and poor old Zeke drowns.

When he gets to heaven, he is completely bewildered and he asks God, "Lord, why didn't you save me?"

In a frustrated voice, God replied, "Zeke! You gotta work with me here! I sent you two boats and a helicopter!"

Why they call it the Wailing Wall

A journalist assigned to the Jerusalem bureau takes an apartment overlooking the famous Wailing Wall. Every day when she looks out, she sees an old man praying vigorously. Intrigued, she goes down and introduces herself to him.

She tells him, "For the last five days I've noticed you praying at the wall. Do you come here every day?"

He tells her, "Yes dat's true. I come here to pray every day, seven days a veek."

She says, "That's wonderful. And how long have you been doing this?"

The old man replies, "I have been coming here to pray every day for the last twenty five years."

"Marvelous. So tell me then, what do you pray for?"

"Vell," he says, "In da morning I pray for world peace and the brotherhood of man. At noon I go home and have a cup of tea. Then I come back and spend all afternoon praying for the eradication of illness and disease from the earth."

The journalist is impressed. She says, "That's amazing. How does it make you feel to come here every day for twenty five years and pray for these things?"

The old man looks at her sadly and says, "Lady, it feels like I'm talking to a frickin' wall."

If there really is a Heaven and a Hell

In Heaven:

The English would be the police.

The French would be the cooks.

The Germans would be the mechanics.

The Italians are the lovers.

The whole place is organized by the Swiss.

In Hell:

The Germans are the police.

The English are the cooks.

The French are the mechanics.

The Swiss are the lovers.

The whole place is organized by the Italians.

A prayer for Brother Leroy

The preacher told his flock, "If there is anyone among you with a special need who wants to be prayed for, please come forward and let us pray for you."

Leroy approached the altar and the preacher asked him, "Brother Leroy, tell the brothers and sisters how our prayers can help you?"

Leroy replied, "Preacher, I need you to pray for help with my hearing."

The preacher put a finger of one hand in Leroy's ear, placed his other hand on top of Leroy's head, and began to pray a "blue streak" for Brother Leroy. At the preacher's urging, the entire congregation enthusiastically joined in.

After a few minutes, the Preacher removed his hands, stood back and asked, "Brother Leroy. How is your hearing now?"

Leroy answered, "I don't know. My hearing ain't 'til next week."

Four Rabbis in Central Park

Four rabbis in New York City would walk together in Central Park where they would engage in deep theological conversations which constantly turned into heated, theological arguments with three of them always in accord against the fourth.

One day, the odd rabbi out, after the usual, "Three to one-majority rules," statement that signified that he had lost again, decided to appeal to a higher authority. Looking to the heavens, he cried out, "Oh, God! I know in my heart that I am right and they are wrong! Could you please give us a sign to prove to them the error of their thinking!"

It was a beautiful, sunny, cloudless day but as soon as the rabbi finished his prayer, a small storm cloud appeared and moved across the sky above them. It rumbled once and then dissolved.

The rabbi turned to the others and said, "A sign from God already! See, I am right. I knew it!"

But the other three disagreed, pointing out that storm clouds like that form quite naturally on hot summer days.

So the rabbi prayed again, "Oh, God, I need a bigger sign to show that I am right and they are wrong. So please, God, this time could I please have just a little bit bigger sign!"

This time, four storm clouds appeared, rushed toward each other to form one big cloud from which a bolt of lightning shot out and slammed into a tree on a nearby hill.

"See! I told you I was right!" cried the rabbi.

But, once again, his friends insisted that nothing had happened that could not be easily explained by natural causes.

The rabbi was getting ready to ask for "this time… a very big sign," but just as he turned to the heavens and said, "Oh God…," the sky turned pitch black, the earth shook, and a deep, booming voice intoned, "How many times do I have to do this? Heeeeeee's totally right you schmucks!"

The rabbi put his hands on his hips, turned to the other three and with a very smug look, said, "Well?"

"Well, what?" shrugged the other rabbis. "It's still only three to two."

Papal humour

A Catholic church in Queens, New York has a raffle. The prize is a trip to Rome to meet the Pope and an old, Italian bricklayer is the winner. His family chips in and buys him a beautiful, three-piece, made-to-measure suit to wear for his Papal meeting.

The man flies to Italy and goes to the Vatican where he is placed in a reception line with about fifty other people. All of them are well dressed except for the man beside the guy from Queens - an unwashed, unshaven derelict who is dressed in the rags of a homeless person.

The Pope proceeds down the reception line; nodding to each person and letting them kiss his ring. He doesn't talk to them though; he just nods and offers his ring.

He does, however, stop at the homeless person, leans over and whispers something to him. When he reaches the end of the line, he turns around and heads back up the line saying his goodbyes and offering his personal blessing - still not talking personally with any of them.

The guy from Queens, wanting to get a more personal greeting from the Pope, turns to the homeless man and offers him one hundred Euros to change clothes with him.

The homeless man readily agrees.

After the switch, the Pope comes along and seeing the guy from Queens—now dressed as the homeless man—walks straight back over to him, bends over and whispers in his ear, "I thought I told you to get the hell out of here."

A rose by any other name

A Spaniard, a Frenchman an Italian and a German are having a few drinks and celebrating the new 'Euro' economy. This eventually morphs into a debate about which of their languages was the most pleasing to the ear.

The Spaniard says, "Consider the word: 'butterfly'. In Spanish, it is pronounced 'Mariposa', a most beautiful sounding word."

The French guy says, "I agree that 'Mariposa' is a very lovely sounding word, but I think that the French word; 'Papillion' sounds even more beautiful to the ear."

The Italian makes his case by saying, "In Italia we hava the mosta beautiful sounding language ina the whola world. The Italiano word for butterfly isa – 'Farfalla.' I thinka that isa the mosta beautiful sounding word of all."

The German guy looks kind of like he has been slighted and says, "Undt vat iss wrong mitt 'Schmetterlink'!?"

A rabbi and a priest

A Jewish Rabbi and a Catholic Priest met at the town's annual Fourth of July picnic. As old friends, they began their usual tongue-in-cheek bantering.

"This baked ham is really delicious," the priest teased the rabbi. "You really ought to try it. I know, I know… it's against the laws of your religion, but I can't understand why such a wonderful food should be forbidden to you by our Lord! You don't know what you're missing. You just haven't lived until you've tried Mrs. Hall's prized Virginia Baked Ham. Come on Rabbi, when are you going to break down and try it?"

The rabbi looked at the priest with a big grin, and said, "At your wedding."

Talk about thrifty!

Duncan drops by his pal Clyde's place one Saturday afternoon for a wee bit o' Scotch and finds Clyde stripping the wallpaper of his living room walls.

"I see ye'r finally redecoratin'," he tells him.

Clyde looks at him and says, "Nae laddie. I'm movin'."

The traditional recipe for "Chicken à la Soprano?"

First… you whack the chicken.

The Texas mafia

Down around the Texas-Louisiana border, there had been a recent rash of illegal cock fighting along with quite a bit of gambling – also illegal. The director of the Louisiana State Police finally bent to public pressure and sent an investigator to get to the bottom of the problem.

The investigator, a fellow named Boudreaux, took an unmarked cruiser and headed for Mamou. He was gone for two days and when he arrived back in Baton Rouge to report to the director, he reported that there were three major groups involved in the illegal cock fighting – Texas Aggies, Cajuns and the Mafia.

Of course, the boss wanted to know how he had deduced this.

The investigator replied that he knew there were Texas Aggies involved when he saw someone enter a duck into the fight.

He went on to say that he knew that there were Cajuns involved when someone bet on the duck.

He then stated that he was absolutely positive that the Mafia was involved when the duck won!

A true Scotsman

A Scottish lad and lass were sitting together on a heathery hill in the Highlands. They had been silent for a while when the lass said, "A penny for yer thoughts Angus."

Angus was a bit shy, but he finally said, "Well Mary, I was thinkin' how nice it would be if ye were to give me a wee bit of a kiss."

So… she did.

Soon after, he again lapsed into a pensive mood which lasted long enough for Mary to ask him, "And what are ye thinkin' now Angus?"

Angus replied, "I was hopin' that ye hadn't forgot about the penny!"

The Chinese synagogue

A guy from Brooklyn was strolling around Hong Kong, taking in the sights and was quite surprised to come upon a synagogue. He went in and sure enough, he saw a Chinese rabbi and a Chinese congregation. The service was touching.

When the service ended, the rabbi went and stood at the door greeting his flock. When our Brooklyn friend came up to him, the rabbi asked, "You are Jewish?"

"Yes, I'm Jewish," replied the Brooklyn-ite.

The Chinese rabbi shook his head slowly and said, "Dat bery, bery funny, you don't rook Jewish."

Paddy's accounting test

Paddy had long wanted to be an accountant, so he went for an aptitude test. The tester asked him, "If I give you two rabbits, and two rabbits, and then, another two rabbits, how many rabbits would you have?"

Paddy replied, "Seven!"

The tester was quite surprised by this answer and replied, "No. That's wrong. Now listen carefully: if I give you two rabbits, and then two more rabbits, and then I give you another two rabbits, how many rabbits have you got?"

Again Paddy replied, "Seven!"

The frustrated tester thought for a second and said, "Okay then, let's go at this from another direction. You've got two bottles of beer and I give you two bottles of beer and then… I give you two more bottles of beer, how many bottles of beer have you got?"

Paddy replied, "Six!"

The tester smiled, "Good! That's perfect.

Now… back to square one; if I give you two rabbits, and two rabbits, and then… two more rabbits, how many rabbits have you got?"

Paddy came back with, "Seven!"

The exasperated tester asked, "Paddy! How on earth can you possibly figure that you'd have seven rabbits?"

Paddy very matter-of-factly replied, "Well y'a see, I've already got one rabbit at home!"

Australia's national joke

What do you call a boomerang that won't come back?

A: A stick.

Heard about the Polish Mafia?

They make you an offer you can't understand.

Bin Laden's last Facebook message

"Be right back. Someone's at the door."

Hi-tech's greatest moment

Stanley and Mike are having a few drinks one night and they become involved in a deep discussion about what was the greatest invention of the twentieth century.

Stanley says, "Well, to me anyway, the greatest invention of the twentieth century would have to be the television. It was introduced to the market in 1949 and by 1969, everybody in the world watched a man land on the moon on TV."

Mike says, "Well Stanley, I'll grant you that the TV is definitely a great invention but for me, the greatest invention of the twentieth century would have to be the thermos."

"The thermos!" Stanley said. "What the heck is so great about a plain old thermos?"

Mike says, "Think about it now… if you put something hot in it, it keeps it hot, but if you put something cold in it, it keeps it cold."

"What's so wonderful about that? " Stanley asked.

With a wondrous smile, Mike asked, "How does it know?"

Irish loveliness

Two Irishmen are looking through a mail order catalogue. Paddy says, "Just look at these fine-lookin' gorgeous women in here! And the prices are so reasonable."

Mick agrees and tells Paddy, "I'm ordering one right now"

Three weeks later Paddy says to Mick, "Has your lovely new woman turned up yet?"

"No," said Mick, "but it shouldn't be long now though. Her clothes arrived yesterday."

True Patriot's Love

An American, a Scotsman and a Canadian were in a terrible car accident. They were all brought to the same emergency room, but all three of them died before they arrived. Just as they were about to put the toe tag on the American, he stirred and opened his eyes. The astonished doctors and nurses asked him what happened.

"Well," said the American, "I remember the crash, and then there was a beautiful light, and then the Canadian and the Scot and I were standing at the gates of heaven. St. Peter approached us and said that we were all too young to die, and said that for a donation of $50, we could return to earth. So of course I pulled out my wallet and gave him the $50, and the next thing I knew I was back here."

"That's amazing!" said the one of the doctors, "But what happened to the other two?"

"Last I saw them," replied the American, "the Scot was haggling over the price and the Canadian was waiting for the government to pay."

The supplies guy

An Italian, an Irishman and a Chinese fellow are hired at a construction site. The foreman takes them to a huge pile of sand and tells them that their job is to load the sand into the back of a truck.

He tells the Italian guy, "You're in charge of all the shoveling so you load the sand into the wheelbarrow."

He tells the Irishman, "You're in charge of the wheelbarrow. After he loads it with sand, you take it over and dump it in the back of that truck over there."

Then he turns to the Chinese guy and says, "You my friend, are in charge of supplies."

Then he tells them, "I have to leave for a little while but I expect you guys to have that pile of sand loaded into the back of that truck when I get back."

The foreman returns a few hours and is surprised to find that the pile of sand is untouched and the Italian guy and the Irishman are just standing there twiddling their thumbs.

He asks them, "What the hell's going on here? Why didn't you guys load any of that sand into the wheelbarrow like I told you to do?"

The Italian replies, "I'm a sorry boss but I no gotta da shovel an' you tella me dat Chinese'a guy, he's a supposa bringa da supplies, but he'sa disappear. We canna no find him anywhere. The son om a gun isa justa disappeared!"

The Irishman adds, "That's right sir. We looked all over for that Chinese fella in charge of supplies, but we couldn't find him."

The foreman is really angry now, and storms off looking for the Chinese guy.

After a half hour search proves fruitless, he is getting angrier by the minute.

Suddenly, the Chinese guy springs out from behind the pile of sand and yells... "Supplies!!"

A blonde pilot

It seems that a young blonde man volunteered for military service during World War II. Despite being blonde, he had such a high aptitude for aviation that he was immediately sent straight to Pensacola… skipping boot camp altogether.

The very first day at Pensacola he solos and is the best flier on the base. All they could do was give him his gold wings and assign him immediately to an aircraft carrier in the Pacific.

On his first day aboard he took off and single-handedly shot down six Japanese Zeroes. Then climbing up to twenty thousand feet, he found nine more Japanese planes and shot them all down, too.

Noting that his fuel was getting low, he descended, circled the carrier and came in for a perfect landing on the deck. He threw back the canopy, climbed out and jogged over to the captain.

Saluting smartly he said, "Well sir, how did I do on my very first day?"

With an evil smile smiled, the captain replied, "Nota bad younga man. But… you make one velly, velly big mistake!"

Irish death notice

Mrs. Murphy was chatting over the back yard fence to Mrs. O'Brien. "Did you hear Mrs. Flynn's husband passed away last night?"

"No!" said Mrs. O'Brien, "was it the cancer?"

Shaking her head gravely, Mrs. Murphy replied, "Oh no. It wasn't anything that serious."

A true Englishman

A Swiss guy, looking for directions, pulls up at a bus stop where two Englishmen are waiting.

"Entschuldigung, koennen Sie Deutsch sprechen?" he says.

The two Englishmen just stare at him.

"Excusez-moi, parlez vous Francais?"

The two continue to stare.

"Parlare Italiano?"

No response,

"Hablan ustedes Espanol?"

Still nothing.

As the Swiss guy drives off, extremely frustrated, the first Englishman turns to the second and says, "You know, maybe we should learn a foreign language...."

"What for?" says the other, "That bloke knew four languages, and it didn't do him any good at all."

Revenge from beyond

An elderly Jewish woman decided to have her portrait painted. She told the artist, "I want you to paint me with diamond earrings, a diamond necklace, emerald bracelets and a ruby broach. Oh yes, and a solid gold Gucci watch too."

"But… you are not wearing any of those things," replied the artist.

"I know," she said. "It's in case I should die before my husband. I'm sure he will remarry his young girlfriend right away, and I want that little tramp to go crazy looking for the jewelry."

David Letterman on Americans

"America is a country where a significant proportion of the population believes that professional wrestling is real but the moon landing was faked."

How the Italians do business

Carmine tells his son at his college graduation, "I have a nice girl picked out for you to marry."

His son Vito, tells him, "Papa... please don't try to make me do this. I will choose my own bride!!!"

Carmine tells him, "'But the girl is Bill Gates' daughter!"

Vito thinks about that for a few seconds and then tells his father, "Well, in that case... okay."

Next Carmine approaches Bill Gates and tells him, "I have a husband for your daughter."

Bill Gates tells him, "But my daughter is far too young to even consider marriage!"

Carmine tells him, "But Bill, this young man is a vice-president of the World Bank."

Gates smiles and tells him, "Ah, in that case... it's a deal!"

Finally Carmine goes to see the president of the World Bank and tells him, "I have a young man to be recommended as a vice-president for you bank."

The president of the World Bank tells him, "But I already have more vice- presidents than I need!"

Carmine tells him, "But this young man is Bill Gates' son-in-law!"

The World Bank president tells him, "Well in that case... okay!"

An atheist gets religion

An atheist was spending a quiet day fishing when suddenly his boat is attacked by the Loch Ness monster. With one simple flip of its tail, the beast tosses the fisherman and his boat high in the air. The beast then opened its mouth and waited for the guy to fall in.

As the man flew through the air, he cried out, "Oh God! Please help me!"

All of a sudden, the horrible attack scene froze in place, and as the atheist hangs in mid-air, a voice booms down from the heavens, "What's with the, 'Oh God?' I thought you didn't believe in me."

The guy says, "Cut me a little slack here please. Twenty seconds ago, I didn't believe in the Loch Ness monster either."

Learning to communicate

A blonde woman and her blonde husband were delighted when their long wait to adopt a baby came to an end: the adoption center called and told them that they had a wonderful Russian baby boy for them.

The couple took him without hesitation.

On the way home from the adoption center, they decided to stop by the local community college so they could enroll in night courses.

After they filled out the forms, the registration clerk inquired, "What ever possessed you to want to learn Russian?"

The couple said proudly, "Well we just adopted a Russian baby and in a year or so he's going to start talking. We just want to be able to understand him."

A nun's story

It is very late at night as two nuns are driving through a cemetery in France. Suddenly there is a tremendous crash as a large, ugly vampire drops down out of a tree and lands on the hood of their car.

A very frightened Sister Agnes tells Sister Mary Catherine, "Sister Agnes... save us! Show him your cross!"

Sister Agnes rolls down her window leans out and looks the vampire right in the eye and in a very angry voice she yells at him, "Get the hell off our car!"

A Christian insult

A guy was getting ready to tee off on the first hole when a second golfer approached and asked if he could join him.

The first man said that he usually played alone, but agreed to the twosome.

They were even after the first two holes and the second guy said, "We're about evenly matched, how about playing for five bucks a hole?"

The first guy said that he wasn't much for betting, but in order to a good sport decided to agree to the terms.

The second guy won the remaining sixteen holes with ease.

As they were walking back to the clubhouse, the second guy was busy counting his $80.00. He confessed that he was the pro at a neighboring course and liked to pick on suckers.

The first fellow revealed that he was the local parish priest.

The pro was flustered and apologetic, offering to return the money.

The priest said, "No way my son, you won fair and square and I was foolish to bet with you. You keep your winnings."

The pro said, "Well father, is there anything I can do to make it up to you?"

The priest said, "Well, you could come to Mass on Sunday and bring your mother and father along. I'd be happy to marry them."

Mark Twain on faith

"Faith is believing in something you just know ain't true."

Archie Bunker on faith

"It ain't supposed to make sense; it's faith. Faith is something that you believe that nobody in his right mind would believe."

Archie Bunker on revenge

"There's nothing wrong with revenge. It's the best way to get even."

The sensitive Scottish guy

A Scotsman and his wife were out for a leisurely stroll and they walked past a swanky new restaurant.

"Oh Angus mah darlin' can ye smell all that wonderful food?" she asked. "It smells absolutely incredible!"

Being a kind-hearted and sensitive Scotsman, he thought to himself, "What the heck... I'll give her a little treat!"

So, they walked past it again.

The Irish lottery winner

An Irish fella won big on the national lottery. He phoned the head office and asked when his winnings would arrive. They told him it would be at least three weeks before they could get the cheque out to him.

"Three weeks!" exclaimed the Irish fellow. "Oh, to hell with that, I say. I want my money back!"

Classic Catskill standup lines

* "I just got back from a pleasure trip. I took my mother-in-law to the airport."

* "Someone stole all my credit cards but I won't be reporting it. So far the thief is spending less than my wife did."

* "My wife and I went back to the hotel where we spent our wedding night; only this time I stayed in the bathroom and cried."

* "The Doctor called Mrs. Cohen saying, 'Mrs. Cohen, your check came back.' Mrs. Cohen answered, 'So did my arthritis!'"

Outsmarting God?

This guy is talking to God and he asks, "Hey God, what is a million years like to you?"

God says, "It's like a second."

The guy then asks, "Well then, what is a million dollars like to you?"

God says, "It's like a nickel."

The guy then asks, "God, could I please have a nickel?"

God says, "Sure, just a second."

And the Lord didst sayeth unto John

"Come forth and ye shall receive eternal life."

But sadly, John came in fifth and all he won was a toaster.

Steven Weinberg

"With or without religion you have good people doing good things and evil people doing evil things, but for good people to do evil things... that takes religion."

Anonymous

The fact that there's a highway to hell and only a stairway to heaven says a lot about anticipated traffic numbers.

A redneck's last words

"Hey guys. Watch this."

Chapter 7

Senior Moments

Helen Hayes (at age 84)

"The hardest years in life are those between ten and seventy."

How to deal with a bad memory

While at his friend's home for dinner, Bernie noticed that Morris, the host, preceded every request to his wife with endearing terms. He called her Honey, My Love, Darling, Sweetheart, etc.

Finally he looked at Morris and remarked, "That is so nice, that after all these years of being married, you keep calling your wife those pet names."

Morris hung his head and whispered, "Don't spread this around but I forgot her name three years ago."

Your grandmother will love this

A man was taking a flight from Atlanta to Miami. An older lady is seated beside him and she is reading her bible.

As she sat there beside him reading the bible, he chuckled and said to her, "You don't really believe all that stuff in there do you?"

She replied, "Of course I do! After all, this is the Bible… the word of God."

He said, "Are you telling me that you actually believe that Jonah was swallowed by a whale and then lived to tell about it?"

She replied, "Of course I do! It says so in the Bible."

Then he asked, "So you actually believe that he survived all that time actually living inside a whale?"

"I most certainly do. Like I said, it's in the bible."

"Well how do suppose he did it?"

She replied, "I don't really know how he did it. I suppose when I get to heaven I'll ask him."

With a sarcastic sneer he said, "Oh yeah. Well what if he's not in heaven?"

With the sweetest of smiles, she turned to him and said, "Well in that case, you can ask him."

151

Why you shouldn't lie about your age

A lady is having a bad day at the roulette tables in Las Vegas. Down to her last $50 and totally exasperated, she exclaims, "What rotten luck I'm having! What number should I play now?"

A man standing next to her suggests, "Why don't you play your age?" (pays 36 to 1)

She smiles at him, "Thanks, that's a great idea."

He wishes her good luck and walks away. Moments later, he hears a loud commotion at the roulette table. *"Maybe she won!"* he thinks to himself.

He rushes back to the table and pushes his way through the crowd to find the lady lying limp on the floor, with the table operator kneeling over her.

The man is stunned and he asks, "What happened?"

The operator replied, "I don't know. She put all her money on 29, and when 36 came up she just fainted!"

Dazed and confused

An older guy is driving down the freeway when his car phone rings. His wife was calling, "Sweetheart, I just heard on the news that there's some guy driving the wrong way on I-94. I know that's the way you come home so please be careful."

He tells her, "Darling. It's not just one car. There are hundreds of them!"

The tragedies of the aging process

First you forget names. Then you forget faces. Then you forget to zip up your fly. But the real tragedy is when you forget to unzip it!

Forgetting

Two older couples are out for an evening walk. The ladies are walking together ahead of the men; Fred and Ralph.

Fred tells Ralph, "We had dinner in a wonderful restaurant last night; superb food and great prices too."

Ralph says, "Sounds like a great spot. Gladys and I are always looking for new places to eat. What was the name of it?"

Fred says, "You know Ralph, my memory is not what it used to be. You're going to have to help me out here. What's the name of that very pretty flower that smells so sweet and grows on a real thorny bush?"

Ralph pauses to think for a few seconds and then says, "Could it be a rose?"

Fred smiles as the word finally comes back into his mind, "A rose. Yes, that's it… a rose."

Fred looked ahead toward his wife and yelled out, "Hey Rose! What was the name of that nice restaurant where we had dinner last night?"

How priorities change as you get older

After an afternoon of golf, four guys are sitting at the bar having a few. Three of the guys were in their forties but the fourth was well into his seventies. After their second drink, the subject of which actress they would most like to be stuck with in an elevator came up.

The three younger men named three sexy, ravishing actresses and then turned to the older man to see who he would name. He replied, "The one who knows how to fix elevators."

Forget me not

A couple in their late eighties began to experience problems remembering things so they decided to go to their doctor and tell him about their predicament. After a thorough battery of tests, the doctor tells them that they were physically okay but that it would be a good idea to start writing things down; "making notes to help you remember things."

Later that night while watching TV, the old man gets up out of his chair and his wife asks, "Where are you going?"

He replies, "To the kitchen."

She asks, "Well… while you're there, would you please get me a bowl of ice cream?"

He replies, "Sure."

She tells him, "You might want to write that down so you can remember it?"

"No, I can remember that."

She adds, "Well then, I would also like some strawberries on top. You had better write that down. Remember what the doctor told us."

He says, "I can remember that. You want a bowl of ice cream with strawberries."

She replies, "Well, I also would like some whipped cream on top.

Now you'd better write that down because I know you'll forget that."

With a touch of irritation in his voice, he tells her, "I don't need to write it down. I can remember that."

So, off he goes to the kitchen and about twenty minutes later, he returns and hands her a plate of bacon and eggs.

She stares at the plate for a moment and then says, "See! I told you to write it down you old fart! You forgot my toast!"

The meaning of life

A man in a restaurant notices a waitress pushing a cart with a huge birthday cake – totally covered with candles. After she delivers it to a large table, the man goes over to the waitress and asks, "Excuse me ma'am, but would you mind telling me just what that cake with all those candles was all about?"

"Certainly sir," she replied. "The gentleman at the end of the table is celebrating his 104th birthday."

The man is shocked. "That guy is a hundred and four? That's incredible! He doesn't look anywhere near that age."

Unable to suppress his curiosity, he walks over to the table and after introducing himself, he congratulates the man on his remarkable achievement. Then he says, "I don't mean to pry sir, but would you mind telling me just exactly what your secret is. You're in fantastic shape yet you're 104 years old. How can that be?"

The young-looking old man replies, "That's an easy one son. Ever since I was born, I have never eaten meat, only fish and pure organic fruits and vegetables. I only drink spring water and pure fruit juices. I have never smoked, drank liquor or done drugs - not even an aspirin. I've never even had sex! I get up at 6 a.m. and I go to bed at 7 p.m. I run five miles every morning and work out for two hours every afternoon."

"And that is why you are 104 years old?"

With a very sad face, the man replied, "No son… that's not why… that's *how*. I still don't know why."

Old people watching out for each other

Henry and Martha had been married for many years and were now in their late 70's. Lately Henry had become a little worried about Martha. He had noticed that she seemed to be losing her hearing so, he decided to conduct a little test to see just how bad her hearing really was.

He stood about fifteen feet behind her in the kitchen and in his normal voice, he asked her, "Martha dear, what are we having for dinner?"

There was no response.

He moved a few feet closer and again he asked, "Martha dear, what are we having for dinner?"

Again, there was no response.

This time he moved in closer so that he was about a foot behind her. In his normal speaking voice, he again asked, "Martha dear, what are we having for dinner?"

Martha turned around to face him and with an exasperated look on her face, she said, "Henry! Have you gone deaf or something? For the third time now, we're having roast beef!"

A senior's priorities

Ethel and Martha, two elderly ladies, ran into each other at a laundromat. After inquiring about each other's health, Martha asked Ethel how her husband was doing.

"Oh! Haven't you heard? Ted died last week."

"Really," Martha said. "I'm so sorry to hear that. How did it happen?"

Ethel replied, "Well, he went out to the garden to dig up a cabbage for dinner, had a massive heart attack and just dropped down dead… right there in the middle of the vegetable patch!"

Martha said, "Oh dear! That's terrible. What did you do?"

Ethel replied, "I opened a can of peas instead."

It's always something

The wife asked her seventy-five year old husband, "How was your golf game, dear?"

He replied, "Well, I was hitting the ball pretty well today, but my eyesight's so bad that I couldn't see where the darned thing went."

"Well darling. You are seventy-five years old," she said. "Why don't you take my brother Scott, along?"

"But he's eighty-five and doesn't even play golf anymore," he protested.

"That may be, but he's got perfect eyesight. He can watch your ball for you."

Well, the guy couldn't argue with that: it seemed like a fine idea. So... the next day, he teed off with his brother-in-law Scott, looking on.

At the first tee, after a powerful swing, the ball disappeared way down the middle of the fairway.

"Do you see where it went?" he asked.

"Yup," Scott answered as he stood there gazing down the fairway.

"Well, where is it?"

Scott turned to him and with a sad and bewildered look on his face replied, "I forget."

Why old men don't get hired

Walt, a seventy year old man is being interviewed for a job as a greeter at Wal-Mart. The interviewer asks him, "So Walt, what do you think is your greatest weakness?"

Walt takes a minute to think about that and then says, "Well I think my greatest weakness is honesty."

The interviewer says, "Well I certainly don't think honesty could ever be considered a weakness."

Walt replies, "Honestly... I don't give a shit what you think."

The Geezer Clinic

An old retired farmer was very bored and decided to open a medical clinic. He put a sign up that said: Dr. Geezer's clinic. Treatment $500. If you are not cured you get back $1,000.

Doctor "Young," who was positive that this old timer had no idea about medicine, thought this would be a great way to make $1,000 so he went to Dr. Geezer's clinic.

He told Dr. Geezer, "I have lost all taste in my mouth. Can you help me?"

Dr. Geezer replied, "Certainly. Nurse, please bring medicine from box 22 and put 3 drops in Dr. Young's mouth."

Dr. Young swallowed the medicine and said, "Aaarrgh !! This is gasoline!"

Dr. Geezer said, "Congratulations! You've got your taste back. That will be $500."

Dr. Young was embarrassed by this and he returned after a couple of days figuring to recover his money. He told Dr. Geezer, "I've lost my memory, I cannot remember anything."

Dr. Geezer smiled and said, "No problem at all. Nurse, please bring medicine from box 22 and put 3 drops in the patient's mouth."

Doctor Young said, "Oh no you don't… that's gasoline!"

Dr. Geezer told him, "Well congratulations! You've got your memory back. That will be $500."

Now Dr. Young is really mad at himself and even more determined to get this guy. He returns after several days claiming, "My eyesight is weak. I can hardly see."

Dr. Geezer said, "Well, I don't have any medicine for that so here's your $1000 back."

Dr. Young counts out the money and says, "Hey… wait a minute… this is only $500."

Dr. Geezer smiled and said, "Congratulations! You got your vision back! That will be $500."

Farting in church

An elderly couple Ethel and Marv were recently attending church. About halfway through the service, Ethel took a pen and paper out of her purse, wrote a note and handed it over to Marv. The note said: "I just let go with a silent fart, what do you think I should do?"

Marv scribbled a quick note on the back of it and handed it back to her. The note read: "Put a new battery in your hearing aid."

Instead of counting years, count your blessings

A group of senior citizens were exchanging comments about their various ailments and infirmities.

Ethyl says, "My arm is so weak I can hardly hold this coffee cup."

Beatrice said, "My cataracts are so bad I can't see to pour coffee."

Mildred added, "I can't turn my head because of the arthritis in my neck."

Winifred says, "My blood pressure pills make my dizzy."

Then Ethyl philosophically replies, "Well… I guess that's the price we pay for getting old."

Beatrice, ever the optimist, adds, "But… it's not all bad. We should at least all be thankful that we can still drive."

Memories

Two very elderly ladies were enjoying the sunshine on a park bench in Miami. They had been meeting in that park every sunny day, for over twelve years; chatting and just enjoying each other's friendship.

One day, the younger of the two ladies, turns to the other and says, "Please don't be upset with me, dear, but I am very embarrassed that after all these years, I can't remember your name. I am trying so hard to remember it, but I just can't."

The older friend, looking very distressed, stares at her but, says nothing for a full five minutes. Finally, with tearful eyes, she turns to her friend and asks, "How soon do you have to know?"

How to freak out an old guy

An old man walks into the barbershop for a shave and a haircut. He tells the barber he can't get all his whiskers off because his cheeks are wrinkled from age. The barber gets a little wooden ball from a cup on the shelf and tells him to put it inside his cheek to spread out the skin. The man does so and the barber starts to shave him.

When he's finished, the old man tells the barber that was the cleanest shave he's had in years but he wanted to know what would have happened if he had accidentally swallowed that little ball.

The barber replied, "Just bring it back in a couple of days like everyone else does."

Vanity - thy name is woman

A sixty-year old woman suffers a heart attack and is taken by ambulance to the hospital. While she is on the operating table, she has a near-death experience. She actually is clinically dead but miraculously, the doctors brought her back to life. During this experience she actually saw God.

She asked him, "Is this it?"

God says, "No way. You have another 36 years left."

So, when she recovered, she decided to stay in the hospital and have plastic surgery; a face lift, collagen implants, liposuction, breast augmentation... the full Monty. She figured that since she had another thirty six years to go, she might as well get the most out of it. Unfortunately, as she was leaving the hospital after her cosmetic surgeries, she was struck by a bus and killed instantly.

Arriving in front of God, she said, "Would you mind telling me just what the heck is going on here? You said I had 36 years to go."

God looked closely at her… then replied, "I'm sorry Evelyn! I didn't recognize you!"

Grandma's Christmas visit

A school bus driver stops to pick up a five-year old boy and he notices an older woman hugging the child before he boards the bus.

Touched by the sight, he asks the boy as he boards, "Is that your grandmother?"

"Yep! She's here to visit us for Christmas."

The driver asked, "Awww… that's so nice. Where does she live?"

"At the airport," the boy replied.

"The airport?" replied the driver.

"Yes sir," the little boy said. "Whenever we want her, we just go there and get her."

Geriatric surgery

An older gentleman was on the operating table awaiting surgery. His son, a renowned cardiac surgeon, would perform the operation.

As he was about to get the anesthesia, he asked to speak to his son.

"Yes, Dad, what is it?"

"Don't be nervous my son. Just do your best, and remember… if it doesn't go well… if something should happen to me, your mother is going to come and live with you and your wife… forever!"

A cute little old lady and her jigsaw puzzle

A little, old silver-haired lady calls her neighbor and says, "Please come over here and help me. I have this killer jigsaw puzzle, and I can't figure out how to even get started."

Her neighbor asks, "What is it supposed to be when it's finished?"

The little silver haired lady says, "According to the picture on the box, it's a rooster."

Her neighbor decides to go over and help with the puzzle. She lets him in and takes him to where she has the puzzle spread all over the table.

He studies the pieces for a moment, then looks at the box, then turns to her and says, "First of all, no matter what we do, we're not going to be able to assemble these pieces into anything resembling a rooster."

He takes her hand and says, "Secondly, I want you to relax. I think we should have a nice cup of tea, and then you and I will put all the Corn Flakes back in the box."

"Will I live to be 80?"

A lady is undergoing her annual physical with a new doctor... Doctor Vinnie Boombatz who told her she was doing, "fairly well" for her age.

A little concerned about that comment, she couldn't resist asking him," Do you think I'll live to be 80?"

Dr. Vinnie asked, "Do you smoke or drink beer or wine or liquor?"

"Oh no," she replied. "I've never done drugs, either."

Then he asked, "Do you eat rib-eye steaks and barbecued ribs?"

"No, my last Doctor told me that red meat is very unhealthy."

Dr. Vinnie asked, "Do you spend a lot of time in the sun, you know like playing golf, sailing, hiking, or bicycling?"

"No, I don't," she said.

He asked, "Do you gamble, drive fast cars, or have a lot of sex?"

"No," she said. "I don't do any of those things."

Dr. Vinnie looked at her and asked, "Then why would you ever want to live that long."

Warren Buffett meets a really smart guy

Warren Buffet goes to meet an old friend of his for lunch. His friend is seventy-five years old so Warren is quite surprised when his friend shows up accompanied by a gorgeous, young woman. Warren is even more surprised when he introduces her to him as his wife.

During the lunch, the young wife excused herself to go to the ladies room and Warren took this opportunity to ask his friend about his new wife, "Your new young wife is very beautiful," he said. "How old is she?"

Smiling, the friend replied, "She's only twenty five."

Warren, by now quite curious, asks him, "How does a seventy five year old bird like you, convince a beautiful twenty five year old woman like her to marry him?"

"Simple," the smiling friend replied. "I lied about my age."

Warren replied, "Really. That's interesting... very interesting. How old did you tell her you were?"

With a bigger smile, his friend replied, "Ninety seven."

Sad but true

An old guy (not in the best of shape) was working out in the gym when he spotted a good looking young woman who was also working out. He asked the trainer, "What machine in here should I use to impress that gorgeous young lady over there?"

The trainer looked him up and down and said, "I think you'd have your best shot if you tried the ATM in the lobby"

Don't ask, don't tell

Now that they are retired, Fred and Ethyl are discussing all aspects of their future. "What will you do if I die before you do?" Fred asks.

After some thought, Ethyl said that she'd probably look for a house-sharing situation with three other single or widowed women who might be a little younger than herself, since she is so active for her age.

Then Ethyl asked Fred, "What will you do if I die first?"

With a lecherous smile, Fred replied, "Probably the same thing."

Out of the mouths of babes

A young girl and her little brother approach their grandfather and he asks him, "Grampa, would you please make a frog noise?"

The Grampa says, "No."

The little boy goes on, "Aw common... please Grampa... please make a frog noise."

The Grampa says, "No, now go and play."

As the little boy and his sister walk away, he tells her, "You go back and ask Grampa to make a frog noise. He won't do it for me but I think he likes you better than me. Maybe he'll do it for you"

So the little girl goes to her Grampa and says, "Can you please make a frog noise Grampa."

The Grampa says, "I just told your brother no, and now I'm telling you no."

The little girl says, "Aw cummon... please Grampa, please make a frog noise."

The Grampa says, "Why is it so important to you and your brother that I make a frog noise?"

The little girl replied, "Because Mommy said that when you croak, we can go to Disney World!"

Johnny and his grampa

Johnny is sitting by his grandfather's side listening to him talk about the differences between their generations, "When I was a boy my momma would send me down to the corner store with a dollar and I'd come back with 5 potatoes, 2 loaves of bread, three quarts of milk, a hunk of cheese, a box of tea and six eggs."

Johnny says, "Well gramps, we would never do that today... too many security cameras. "

The old fisherman and the talking frog

It seems an old fisherman stumbled across a talking frog while out fishing one day. The frog said, "I'll turn into a ravishing beauty and fulfill your every desire, if you'll only just kiss me."

The fisherman scooped up the frog and put him in his pocket.

Later on, at a bar, he pulled the frog out and set the frog next to his beer. When the bartender overheard the frog repeat the offer, he asked the fisherman, "That sounds like a pretty good deal. Are you going to go for it?"

The old fisherman replied, "Nope. At my age, I'd rather have a talking frog."

Losing your keys

A woman left a meeting at a hotel and gave herself a personal pat down; looking for her keys. They were not in her pockets. A quick search in the meeting room revealed nothing. With a sinking feeling, she realized she must have left them in the car.

Frantically, she headed for the parking lot; her husband had been constantly on her case for leaving the keys in the ignition. Her defense for doing so was that the ignition was the best place not to lose them.

His argument was that that was stupid since the car could easily be stolen.

As she burst through the door, she came to a terrifying conclusion.

His theory was right. The parking lot was empty. She immediately called the police, gave them her location, confessed that she had left her keys in the car, and that it had been stolen. Then she made the most difficult call of all, "Honey," she stammered, "I left my keys in the car, and it has been stolen."

There was a period of uncomfortable silence. She thought the call had been dropped, but then she heard his voice as he yelled at her through gritted teeth, "You crazy old broad! I dropped you off!"

Now it was her time to be silent. Embarrassed but trying to recover some small scrap of dignity, she replied, "Well then, would you please come and get me."

In a very sarcastic tone of voice, he replied, "Why I'd be happy to my dear – as soon as I convince this policeman who is trying to arrest me that I didn't steal your car."

The anonymous *truth* about aging

At 20 – we worry about what others think of us.

At 40 – we don't care about what others think of us.

At 60 – we discover they haven't been thinking about us at all!

The saga of Ralph and Edna

Ralph and Edna were both patients in a mental hospital. One day while they were walking past the hospital swimming pool, Ralph suddenly jumped into the deep end. He sank to the bottom of the pool and stayed there.

Edna promptly jumped in to save him. She swam to the bottom and pulled him out.

When the Director became aware of Edna's heroic act she immediately ordered her to be discharged from the hospital, as she now considered her to be mentally stable. When she went to tell Edna the news she said, "Edna, I have good news and bad news. The good news is you're being discharged, since you were able to rationally respond to a crisis by jumping in and saving the life of the person you love... I have concluded that your act displays sound mindedness.

The bad news is that Ralph hung himself in the bathroom with his bathrobe belt right after you saved him. I am so sorry to have to tell you this, but Ralph is dead."

Edna laughed as she replied, "He didn't hang himself, I just hung him in there to dry."

A real 21st century senior

During his physical examination, a doctor asked his patient, a retired businessman, about his physical activity level. The man told him, "Well, yesterday was a typical day for me. I took a four hour walk covering about five miles over some pretty rough terrain. I waded along the edge of a lake. I pushed my way through several thickets of brambles. I got lots of sand in my shoes and eyes. I almost stepped on a snake and even got chased by an alligator. I climbed several rocky hills and I even took a few leaks behind some trees. The mental stress of it all left me quite shattered so at the end of it all, I drank eight beers."

Impressed by the story, the doctor said, "Boy, you must be one hell of an outdoorsman."

"Not at all," replied the senior. "I'm just a lousy golfer."

Eating crow

While on a road trip, an elderly couple stopped at a roadside restaurant for lunch. After finishing their meal, they left the restaurant and resumed their trip.

The elderly woman unknowingly left her glasses on the table but she didn't miss them until after they had been driving about twenty minutes. By then, to add to the aggravation, they had to travel quite a distance before they could find a place to turn around in order to return to the restaurant to retrieve her glasses.

All the way back, the elderly husband became the classic grouchy old man. He fussed and complained and scolded his wife relentlessly during the entire return drive. The more he chided her, the more agitated he became; he just wouldn't let up for even one minute. To her relief, they finally arrived back at the restaurant.

As the woman got out of the car and hurried inside to retrieve her glasses, the old geezer yelled after her, "While you're in there, would you mind grabbing my hat and my credit card?"

Maxine on being old

"I finally figured out what I want to be when I get older. I want to be younger!"

Two wolves: a good one to tell your grandkids

One evening an old Cherokee told his grandson about a battle that goes on inside each person. He said, "My son, the battle is between two wolves inside each of us; one is evil – it is anger, envy, jealousy, sorrow, regret, greed, arrogance, self-pity, guilt, resentment, inferiority, lies, false pride, superiority, and ego.

The other is good – it is joy, peace, love, hope, serenity, humility, kindness, empathy, generosity, truth, compassion and faith."

The grandson thought about it for a minute and then asked his grandfather: "Which wolf wins?"

The old Cherokee simply replied, "The one you feed."

Senior dating

Ethyl, an energetic 85-year old woman goes on a blind date with a 90 year old guy. When she gets back to the senior's residence her roommate Mavis asks her how it went.

Ethyl told her, "It was terrible. I had to slap his face three times!"

"Really," Mavis said, "did he try to get fresh with you?"

Ethyl says, "No... I though he was dead."

Three seniors are out for a stroll.

One of them remarks, "It's windy."

Another one replies, "No way man. It's Thursday."

The last one says, "Me too. Let's go get a beer."

Deep Thoughts of A Retiree's Wandering Mind

* I had amnesia once --- maybe twice.
* Never do card tricks in front of the people you play poker with.
* Getting lucky now means coming out of a mall and finding my car.
* Money isn't everything but it keeps the kids in touch.
* I'm supposed to respect my elders but it's getting harder and harder for me to find one now.
* You're never too old to learn something stupid.
* Experience is the thing you have left when everything else is gone.
* Instead of looking for the fountain of youth, l should have looked for the fountain of smart.
* We are all born naked, wet and hungry. Then things go downhill.

How seniors have fun in the residence

A sign tacked up on the wall of the dining hall:

There's a guy in here whose name is Jim,

And I just love throwing tomatoes at him,

Now I know you think tomatoes are soft and don't hurt the skin,

But these suckers do, cuz they're still in the tin.

George Burns on aging

* Happiness is having a large, loving, caring, close-knit family… in another city.

* I personally stay away from natural foods. At my age I need all the preservatives I can get.

* I honestly think it is better to be a failure at something you love than to be a success at something you hate.

* If you live to be a hundred, you've got it made. Very few people die past that age.

* You can't help getting older but you don't have to get old.

* It's hard for me to get used to these changing times. I remember when the air was clean and sex was dirty.

* Happiness is a good martini, a good meal, a good cigar and a good woman… or a bad woman… depending on just how much happiness you can stand.

Bob Hope on being old

"I don't feel old. I don't feel anything until noon. Then it's time for my nap."

Brian Keelan on being old

"The main problem with old age is that it comes at such a bad time."

Rodney Dangerfield… funny to the end

In April, 2003 Rodney was entering the hospital for neuro surgery and was asked by a reporter how long he would be hospitalized.

He replied: "If all goes well, about a week. If not, about an hour and half."

Sadly, Rodney died 43 days later – just shy of his 83 birthday.

His headstone reads. "There goes the neighborhood"

"It ain't over till it's over!"

Yogi Berra

Paraprasdokians

Definition: A paraprosdokian is a figure of speech in which the latter part of a sentence or phrase is surprising or unexpected in a way that causes the reader or listener to re-frame or reinterpret the first part. It is frequently used for humorous or dramatic effect and they sell a lot of sweatshirts. Basically they're funny. They don't make sense yet at some weird level… they do. Winston Churchill loved them and he would have loved Yogi Berra…

Yogi Berra

My all-time favourite "Yogi" is when his wife asked him where he would like to be buried.

He replied, "I dunno. Surprise me."

Here are some of Yogi's more famous sayings…

* It's tough to make predictions, especially about the future.
* You got to be very careful if you don't know where you're going because you might not get there.
* It's pretty far but it doesn't seem like it
* If people don't want to come out to the ball park, nobody's gonna stop 'em.
* You can observe a lot by just watching.
* A nickel ain't worth a dime anymore.
* When you come to a fork in the road, take it.
* It was impossible to get a conversation going, everybody was talking too much.
* It's like deja-vu, all over again.
* The future ain't what it used to be.
* Nobody goes there anymore. It's too crowded.
* Little League baseball is a very good thing because it keeps parents off the streets.

* The other teams could make trouble for us if they win.
* Nostalgia ain't what it used to be.
* Always go to other people's funerals, otherwise they won't go to yours.
* On the 1973 Mets: "We were overwhelming underdogs."
* On pregame rest: I usually take a 2 hour nap from 1 to 4."
* His batting philosophy: "You can't think and hit at the same time."

A truly classic Yogi

   Phil Rizzuto: "Hey Yogi, I think. We're going the wrong way."
   Yogi Berra: "Yeah, but we're making great time!"

And then there's Stephen Wright

* You can't have everything. Where would you put it?
* I drive way too fast to worry about cholesterol.
* Drink 'til she's cute, but stop before the wedding.
* Borrow money from pessimists. They don't expect it back.
* I intend to live forever - so far, so good.
* I'd kill for a Nobel Peace Prize
* 24 hours in a day. 24 beers in a case. Coincidence?
* I couldn't repair your brakes, so I made your horn louder.
* If swimming is so good for your figure, how do you explain whales?
* Join the Army, meet interesting people. Then kill them.
* OK, so what's the speed of dark?
* A conscience is what hurts when all your other parts feel so good.
* A clear conscience is usually the sign of a bad memory.
* If you want the rainbow, you gotta put up with the rain.
* All those who believe in psychokinesis, raise my hand.
* The early bird may get the worm, but the second mouse gets the cheese.
* If everything seems to be going well, you have obviously overlooked something.
* Depression is merely anger without enthusiasm.
* The more you run over a dead cat, the flatter it gets.
* Hard work pays off in the future, laziness pays off now.

* Why do psychics have to ask you for your name?
* Whenever I think of the past, it brings back so many memories...
* Everything is within walking distance if you have the time.
* Two wrongs don't make a right, but strangely enough, three rights do make a left.
* I was arrested for lip-synching karaoke
* How young can you be to die of old age?
* If god dropped acid, would he see people?
* On the other hand... you have different fingers.
* If you are in a spaceship travelling at the speed of light and you turn on the headlights, would you see anything?
* How can you tell when you run out of invisible ink?
* Why is "Abbreviation" such a long word?

Paraprasdokian - ish

* If you don't have anything good to say about someone, make sure they're not around when you say it.
* If all is not lost, where the heck is it?
* I want to die peacefully in my sleep like my grandfather... not yelling and screaming like the passengers in his car.
* The only thing wrong with a perfect drive to work is that you end up at work.
* I'd like to agree with you, but then we'd both be wrong.
* War does not determine who is right - only who is left.
* Knowledge is; knowing that a tomato is a fruit.
  Wisdom is; not putting it in a fruit salad.
* To steal ideas from one person is plagiarism.
  To steal from many is research.
* You do not need a parachute to skydive. You only need a parachute to skydive twice.
* There are three kinds of people: those who can count and those who can't.
* Indecision is the key to flexibility.
* Where there's a will... I want to be in it.

* If we are here to help others, what are the others here for?
* Why does someone believe you when you say there are four billion stars, but they have to check it out when you say the paint is wet?
* In the sixties, people took acid to make a normal world look weird. Now the world is weird and those same people take Prozac to make it look normal.
* A bank is a place that will lend you money, if you can prove to them that you don't need it.
* Those who live by the sword get shot by those who don't.
* We never really grow up. We only learn how to act in public.
* I didn't say it was your fault. I only said I was blaming you.
* If man evolved from monkeys and apes, why do we still have monkeys and apes?
* The only good thing you can say about an egotist is that they don't talk about other people.
* If you try to fail and succeed, what have you really done?
* Why are hemorrhoids not called asteroids?
* Always remember you're unique... just like everyone else.
* It may be that your sole purpose in life is simply to serve as a warning to others.
* Nothing sucks more than that moment during an argument when you realize you're wrong.
* I keep some people's phone numbers in my phone just so I know not to answer when they call.
* Suburbia is a place where they tear out the trees and then name streets after them.
* When bad turns to worse, you're in trouble but when worse turns to worst... you're totally screwed.
* I am not a perfectionist... but my parents were.
* Every time I find out the meaning of life... they change it.
* I just want revenge... is that so wrong?
* Eat well and stay fit so you can die healthy.
* God is black and boy is she mad.
* God give me patience... and give it to me right now!

Celebrity paraprasdokian - ish quotes

Warren Buffett

"A rich person should leave his kids enough to do something... but not enough to do nothing."

Arthur C. Clarke

"I don't believe in Astrology. I am a Sagittarius and we're very skeptical."

Albert Einstein

"The only reason for time is so that everything doesn't happen at once."

Anonymous

"Can atheists buy insurance for Acts of God?"

Spike Milligan

"The best cure for seasickness is to sit under a tree."

Emo Phillips

* "I asked God for a bike, but then I learned that God doesn't work that way so... I stole a bike and asked for forgiveness."
* "A computer once beat me at chess but it was no match for me at kickboxing."

Johnny Carson

"If life were really fair, Elvis would still be alive and all the impersonators would be dead."

Lily Tomlin

"Why is it that when we talk to God we're said to be praying, but when God talks to us we're schizophrenic?"

Ray Bradbury

"I don't believe in being serious about anything. I think life is too serious to be taken seriously."

Harold Coffin

"Middle age is that awkward period when Father Time catches up with Mother Nature."

About the author

Brian Keelan: aka The QuitSmokingGuy, is the author of: *How To Quit Smoking and Save Your Life* – a book he wrote to teach smokers how to get themselves ready to quit smoking and this book you are now reading which is in it's 2nd edition

Brian has a BA from the University of Western Ontario – majoring in Economics and Philosophy. He spent 4 years in sales with IBM Canada before opening his own consumer electronics retail business: *Keelans Audio Video Centre* which he owned and operated for 32 years before retiring in 2003 to pursue a writing career.

Father of three, grandfather of two, he and Sylvia live together in Bright's Grove, Ontario – on the shores of Lake Huron.

He has written over 100 op-ed articles for First Monday Magazine.

He also writes a series of short stories called: *Bucket Rides.* Since quitting smoking had such a profound impact on his life both from a health and a financial perspective, he has used the money he would have spent on cigarettes to embark on a series of "bucket list" adventures that, "I wouldn't even be alive to experience let alone afford if I hadn't eliminated my addiction to nicotine."

He conducts seminars as well. One for teenagers called: The Truth About Smoking – 10 Things Every Teenager Needs To Know and another quit-smoking bootcamp for smokers called: How To Quit Smoking and Save Your Life… plus a lot of money.

He is also writing, "an action/adventure love story," with the working title: *One Last Cruise.*

"I would love to hear from any of you who have read my book – what worked / what didn't work etc. Any ideas you may have about how to make it more helpful to smokers who are trying to quit would be appreciated."

Please contact me at: www.thequitsmokingguy.com

The Joke Book App

Get the **200 Jokes You Can Tell Anybody** App installed right on your iPhone, iPad or iTouch for free with the purchase of the e-joke book. Just look it up on your iTunes account

A friend of mine read my joke book and said, "Boy, I'd love to have that installed in my iPhone. That way when I'm at a pub and want to tell a joke, I've got instant access to them without being too obvious. It would be cool if you had the jokes listed so that I could earmark my favorites so that I could quickly get at the ones I wanted to use.

It would also be cool if I could maybe even send them on to my friends with a note like, "Here – saw this and thought of you. Please enjoy."

Well I thought that would be a pretty good idea so that's exactly what I have done here with my 200 jokes You Can Tell Anybody APP.

The jokes are handy and with you wherever you take your device and it's easy to send them on to your friends, kids, clients or customers.

People seldom remember what you say but they'll always remember how you make them feel.

This app will make you and everyone you give it to feel good... really good.

#####

Other Works

I smoked for over 40 years and during that time I failed to quit smoking on over 70 different occasions. Then on June 6, 2000 – I smoked my last cigarette... ever! That was over 100,000 cigarettes and well over $40,000 after-tax dollars ago.

After I realized I was out of the woods as far as ever smoking or even wanting to smoke another cigarette was concerned, I became quite curious about why I had finally succeeded so completely this time after failing so many times before.

Much to my surprise, I discovered that the main reason I had succeed at quitting smoking was that I had in fact actually *learned how* to do it.

All the products and programs I had tried in my life had all come with the same 'caveat' – the escape clause if you will – that is, they would all say that in order for their product or program to work for you, you had to be ready to do it. That way, when you failed, as over 90% of all smokers who try to quit do, they can say, "Well, you see, it says right here on the box that in order for this to work you have to be really ready to do it. I guess you just weren't well enough prepared."

I also discovered that there wasn't much useful, street-smart information out there about how to get yourself ready to succeed at quitting smoking forever... until now.

But all smokers should know this one simple fact...

There is nothing more important to your success at quitting smoking forever than preparing yourself to do it. Nothing! Learning how to quit before you try to quit will dramatically increase your chances for success at quitting smoking forever and it will also make quitting smoking a lot easier to do

This is a book that everyone who wants to quit smoking should read before they try to quit smoking. It will teach you what you need to know in order to succeed and then show you how to use that information to help you succeed at quitting smoking.

For some free Videos that will help you get started on your road to a smoke-free life – go to www.thequitsmokingguy.com

The quit smoking math App

This is an app designed to help motivate a smoker who wants to quit smoking. It was an invaluable for helping me in my effort to quit my 40 year addiction to nicotine after over 70 failed attempts.

I used it when I was preparing myself to quit smoking by having it as a constant reminder of how much I had smoked and how much money I had wasted and was wasting on cigarettes.

Then after I smoked my last cigarette I used it to count the *cigarettes I had not smoked* and the *money I had not spent* on cigarettes. Every time I got the urge to smoke I would look at the numbers and the motivation to stay quit would kick in.

You can install this useful app right on your iPhone, iPad or iTouch for only $1.99.

Once it's in there, just click on the "Edit my information" button and put in your own personal smoking stats

– number of cigarettes smoked each day

– number of smokes in a pack

– price per pack (use today's prices because they will never be cheaper)

– the date you started and the date you smoked your last cigarette.

The app will do the rest. You can find it at iTunes.

* * * *

The Bucket Rides

This is a story about something I did that I never would have been able to do if I had not succeeded at quitting smoking forever. After I did succeed and I realized that I had succeeded at something that I never believed I would be able to do, I started to ask myself, "What else can I do that I didn't think I'd ever be able to do?"

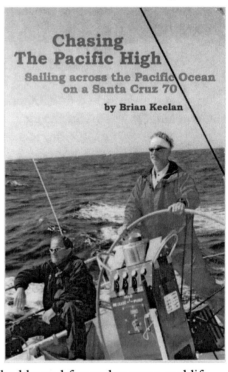

I have been a sailor all my life and I've always wanted to make the trip across the Pacific Ocean on a big fast ocean racing sailboat. I was never good enough to do it as a professional sailor and I was not well-enough connected to be able to convince someone that I would be a useful asset to their crew.

But persistence does pay off and using the money I saved by quitting smoking to fly me out to L.A. I got my wish.

That voyage was everything I had hoped for and more; a real life-affirming experience. This is a 25,000 word short story with pictures that tells you how I got to do it and what it was like.

(In a word… it was great!)

Available as an e-book only at: Amazon Kindle and Smashwords

CPSIA information can be obtained
at www.ICGtesting.com
Printed in the USA
LVOW10s0855140617

538083LV00018B/468/P